The Confident Child
*A Guide to Fostering Personal
Effectiveness in Children*

The Confident Child
A Guide to Fostering Personal Effectiveness in Children

RÉAMONN Ó DONNCHADHA

Newleaf

Newleaf
an imprint of
Gill & Macmillan Ltd
Goldenbridge
Dublin 8
with associated companies throughout the world
www.gillmacmillan.ie
© Réamonn Ó Donnchadha 2000
0 7171 3046 0
Print origination by Carole Lynch
Printed by ColourBooks Ltd

A catalogue record is available for this book
from the British Library.

1 3 5 4 2

CONTENTS

PREFACE

This book is a tool to enable parents and teachers to realise their own potential in the work of enabling and empowering their children. It seeks to do for those who read it what they can also do for the children in their care. If we 'feed the birds in summer', we extinguish their ability to fend for themselves, but if we feed them when they need to be fed, give them enough food, and give them the correct food, we enable them to develop their own capabilities and therefore to survive. If we overprotect our children and over-provide for them, we smother their attempts at assertiveness and prevent them from developing their innate survival skills.

The Effective Child is not a manual setting out a list of rules to be followed in order to produce successful children. It is not a formula that guarantees success, nor is it an easy way of doing the job of parenting or teaching. I have taken some of the more important aspects of the makeup of the person and in each chapter examined how these apply in the life of the child, as well as in the dynamics of the home and the school. Each chapter contains some suggestions and ideas for helping to foster personal effectiveness. These are not commandments written in stone, but rather flexible ideas and guidelines for parents and teachers to apply both in their own lives and in the lives of the children they are responsible for.

The case studies at the end of each chapter are intended to show how the ideas in the book can be put into practice.

The main idea running through the book is that the essential skills necessary for survival are present in our children; and though by cosseting, overprotection and unconscious fear, we are in danger of extinguishing these skills, we have the resources within us to foster and develop these skills. This book is a challenge to the way in which we perceive our children, a challenge to the way in which we pass on what we think is best, and a challenge to the way in which we, as the primary guardians of their future, prepare them for that future.

A note on gender: in the book, the masculine and feminine terms, he/she, his/hers, him/her, etc., are used interchangeably and wherever they occur they can be seen as referring to a boy or a girl, unless specifically noted.

CHAPTER 1
TODAY'S CHILD

When a child is born he comes from the completely secure, comfortable, supportive and safe environment of the mother's womb into a strange, threatening and to him hostile environment. It is the first major separation of the child's life and it is by far the most traumatic that he will experience during the course of many separations in his lifetime. He is dragged from a place where he feels safe and secure into a world where he will feel vulnerable and threatened. The child born into today's world has much to contend with and his parents will have the single greatest influence on what becomes of him. It is his parents who, almost single-handedly, determine both his physical and his psychological makeup.

The job of looking after a child is now perceived to be more complicated and more fraught with risk and uncertainty than it was. At the same time, the combination of a growing industry of information about children and the exaggerated demand for academic success, has undermined the confidence which parents once had in their own innate ability to cater for the needs of their children. This lack of confidence in their own capabilities as parents has two significant effects. Firstly, it lessens their effectiveness as parents; and secondly, this lack of confidence is transmitted to the child in the course of growing up and results in a devaluing of his own sense of capability, making him more dependent on others.

This may be because society has become so much more complex, because people have become more afraid or because children are more vulnerable. I believe that today's child is no more or less vulnerable than his parents; he is no better or worse equipped to cope with what he encounters in life; nor are the dangers he faces greater, relative to his ability to deal with them, than those faced by parents. Different yes, but not greater.

The greater access to information has had a number of implications for both parents and teachers in their dealings with children. Information is now available to everybody, regardless of social status, academic qualification or position in life. This means that parents in particular have access to all the information about children, about behaviour, and about relationships which hitherto was available only to 'experts'. This has both positive and negative effects. Parents can now exercise their right to have access to any information which teachers, psychologists and other professionals may have. This allows them to share the expertise of parents and others engaged in the care of children. The negative side of this is that they may misinterpret what they hear and come to wrong conclusions, or they may attach too much importance to what they read and so devalue their own innate child-rearing skill. The way in which problems are aired and 'solved' on radio and television is a feature of this and tends to impose general solutions on individual problems.

An offshoot of this is the growing tendency to challenge. Of itself this is a welcome trend, but it also means that just as parents are growing less willing to accept information from the 'experts' so children are much less willing to accept that parents, teachers, etc. 'know what is best' for them. It is important that children learn the benefit of being able to challenge, but they also need to feel that their parents 'know what is best', that there are people in their lives who know more than they do and to whom they can turn to in need. The ability to do this helps in the formation of healthy and secure boundaries in the child's life; as we see from the work of Donald Winnicott, secure boundaries are essential to the healthy development of a child.

The greater emphasis on academic success is also a spin-off of this and has led to a greater pressure to absorb the information in the search of higher points. From the moment a child is born the looming spectre of points and college is a defining influence in the way parents treat their children and in the way schools seek to educate them. The excessive importance attached to the end product of college and work is denying the child the process of experiencing childhood.

Another by-product of this information overload has been the over-development of verbal and technological forms of communication, resulting in the neglect and decline of other nonverbal forms of communication. The ability to tune into the feelings of others, to read body language, to listen actively and to express emotions and feelings without fear have all been neglected and are in danger of becoming unused and redundant. The discovery, disclosure and publication of so much abuse, cruelty and mistreatment of adults as children, the great expansion of counselling and therapy services, as well as the greater openness in society regarding disclosure, have contributed to the culture of overprotection.

The process of having children, caring for their needs and of eventually letting them go, is for many parents a process of self-discovery. But parents may feel that if nasty or abusive things could happen to them when they themselves were children, then there is every chance that these same things can happen to their children. The work of Carl Jung has shown how it may be a fear of their own shadow side, an unwillingness to deal with the negative aspects of their own personality and perhaps a mistrust of their own negative self, which is feeding this desire to protect their child from the 'evils of society'. The drive to protect our young is both natural and necessary. The instinct to protect one's future and to take care of one's own offspring is necessary for the healthy development of the child as well as for the psychological well-being of the parent.

It is clear that all abuse should be acknowledged and dealt with and it is necessary that this knowledge should be taken on board in a critical and a balanced way, but as parents and teachers we must guard against overreaction. It is important that current policy in both school and home should take account of what has happened in the past and that it should shape the way we parent and teach our children. But where the normal practice of looking after children and caring for their needs becomes driven by an exaggerated concern for the welfare of the child, this normal caring can become a stifling, smothering overprotection based on the fears of the parent rather than on the needs of the child.

The comprehensive study of child development and personality by American academics Mussen, Conger and Kagan deals extensively with the notion that the child is as much a function of his environment as he is a product of his genetic inheritance. It is clear that because he is influenced both by what he brings with him into the world at birth, i.e. heredity, and by the environment into which he is born and lives, he will grow as a person who will adapt to the pressures and demands of the environment of which he is part.

This does not mean that he can learn to cope without outside intervention. But it does mean that he has the innate capability to cope; all that is required is that he be enabled to use it. His parents and teachers are the facilitators who provide him with the means to use the inner strength that he naturally possesses.

It is true that today's child is faced with a different set of life circumstances than his parents, but it is also true that because he is a product of his own time, he has the capability to develop the required set of coping skills. Overprotection tends to destroy the need for the child to call on his coping skills and therefore, through lack of awareness of the range of coping skills that he has, as well as lack of use of these skills, they become dormant and eventually extinct.

Overprotection is rooted in the feelings of inadequacy and dissatisfaction with the 'self' of the parent or teacher which causes the person to feel threatened by the presence of competence and confidence in others, and makes it difficult for him to accept these traits in others. As a result he may unconsciously seek to prevent these positive traits from growing, developing and being used. It is this unconscious but powerful drive in the adult to maintain his own negative self-view that fights against what it perceives as the threat of seeing competence and confidence in others.

But today's child, while having the innate capabilities to cope with his particular life circumstances, has a quite different set of life situations to those which his parents and his teachers had. This contributes its own specific difficulties. In part, it means that the parent may not have the best angle on what the child needs to survive, but that the child does have. The role of the adult should be to facilitate the growth of the child's latent capabilities, rather than to impose his own skills.

The development of technologically based forms of communication has led to particular effects on children and relationships. The fact that so many homes have a television, a computer, a play station and other types of computer games leads to a number of effects. Children spend increasing amounts of time in 'conversation' with their screen, engaging in one-way conversations, thus denying them access to the affective (feeling) give and take which conversation with another person demands. There is no exchange of language, touch or emotion; the child is interacting with a mechanical device which has no feelings, and so gives out no emotional, tactile or human responses. Interaction with a computer or computer game, gives immediate gratification of needs and a continuous variety of response. Instant gratification means that the child is immediately given the response that he wants and it presents the child with an unrealistic view of reality. Continuous exposure to technological modes of communication and recreation allows the person the luxury of having a conversation with himself where he has complete control over the questions and the answers.

Some of the needs of the child may be easily identified simply by looking at the lifestyle and play habits of children. A salient feature of life for children is the unacceptability of being on their own, playing on their own, or working on their own at home or in school. Perhaps this is the result of genuine parental fears about safety, the notion that it is not healthy to be alone, or an overemphasis on the natural affiliative need that all children usually satisfy by joining in with other children. This has become confused with the belief that children always need to have something to do, that they always have to be amused, preferably with somebody else or with something other than themselves. Consequently, the child never learns — or is never allowed to learn — to be alone or to be happy with his own company. He never learns the value of his own company. This raises the question for the child: 'Is my own company not good enough?' which can lead to the child's sense of self being undermined and undervalued.

Perhaps linked to this is an unexplained fear of shyness and introversion. An introverted person is someone who is quiet, thoughtful and enjoys solitude. He is more interested in ideas than in outside things and people. It is not the same as being shy and is in no sense abnormal or 'wrong'. There may be an unconscious fear that there is something wrong with the child who is quiet and introverted and this sometimes results in a desire to have children always playing with their friends. Parents often worry because their child is shy, introverted or reserved and it often happens that such children do suffer in the competition stakes. But shyness or quietness is not in itself a disadvantage. Such children can learn just as effectively as other, more outgoing children. They learn in a different way and have different needs, but they do not suffer from any disability and do not need to be 'cured'.

Today's child is no better or worse off physically or psychologically, relative to his needs, than his parents were. He has the potential and the capability to survive in his environment, and the role of the parent and teacher is to enable him to use his latent survival skills.

CHAPTER 2
PARENT AND CHILD: MIRROR AND IMAGE

When a child is born, she comes into an environment that predates her. It is a fixed, preset matrix into which she is born. A matrix is a creative, supportive and holding learning environment. The child's parents are already there. Their own physical and psychological makeup is already well established and they will have fixed and clear ideas of who they are and who they want their children to be. Most parents will want a child, will have planned the birth and will already have plans and ambitions for their children. In some cases they will have gone as far as deciding what school the child will go to. The colours in the child's bedroom will have been chosen and the child's name will have been decided. In other words when a child is born her life is already mapped out. And all this happens before the child has even been seen!

When a child is born, she enters a matrix of language, behaviour, expectations, religious belief and values that may or may not be in tune with her genetic makeup at birth, and the unspoken expectation is that she will become a part of this, and that she will become the future carrier of the family's genetic and social inheritance. It is expected that the child will fit into the prefabricated psychosocial niche in society that awaits her, rather than that the environment will change to suit the child.

Though her environment is already established, when the child enters it she will cause change whether the family wants it or not. The balance of power in the family group will alter and the routine of the house will be changed. But to a significant degree the child is a passive participant in all that happens to her. For the most part, it is the child who has to adapt to her surroundings and it is the existing family set up which remains fixed and demands that the child adapt to its demands. Santrock and Yussen's scientifically based work on child development deals extensively with the subject of heredity. It is clear that the child who bears the genetic and archetypal inheritance of her family to begin with is born into an environment that manifests, values and rewards these very traits. So from the very outset, the child is shaped and conditioned in a way that satisfies the family's need to maintain its own self view.

Much work has been done by people such as Stanley Coopersmith, Jerome Kagan and Paul Mussen, detailing the significance of the family environment on the child's thinking, feeling and behaviour in the first five years of life. It is both necessary and inevitable that we as parents want our children to carry on the family traits and characteristics which we value; this reassures us of our own worth, our own self-esteem and our own place in the greater scheme of things. This underlying need to value and maintain our genetic family traits is an unconscious desire to satisfy our need to survive and is essential to the self-esteem and self-image of both parents and children. The more we value ourselves as separate individuals and the more we value our family's genetic traits, the more we will feel that what we have is worth giving to our children. This has added importance, because it also means that we are satisfied that our future is guaranteed in the greater scheme of things.

Much of this self-maintaining is unconscious, which means that to a greater or lesser degree we are shaping our children and rewarding them for the traits which we value in our own psychological makeup, while not being fully aware of what we are doing. It is the unconscious need for validation of our own being which motivates us to praise and encourage our children to reproduce and replicate the behaviours which we deem to have been successful in making us what we are.

So it is therefore both inevitable and necessary that parents will want their children to be like them. To begin with, a certain amount of likeness is inevitable and good, so why question it? The problem arises from the fact that much of this is in reality an unconscious attempt to recreate ourselves. In other words, as the work of Melannie Klein shows, it is more for the maintenance of our own self view that we do this rather than for the 'sake of the children', and it may turn out that it is not the best thing for the particular child in question.

In terms of consciously wanting our children to be like us this happens in the following way. Our religious beliefs, our family values and our general outlook on life are all part of our overall psychological makeup and part of what makes us what we are. The stronger our belief in what and who we are, the more we are likely to want our children to be like us, because we are convinced that if it worked for us and has made us successful, then it is bound to work for the child. At the same time, it will guarantee our stake in the future. The modes of behaviour, language, social and academic expectations of the home will reflect the things we value and children will be rewarded or punished according to how well they fulfil our expectations.

We will naturally reward them for the behaviour that meets with our approval and we will punish, or at least discourage, them for behaviour we don't agree with. In other words, we will encourage that behaviour which we want, or which satisfies our unconscious need for survival, and we will discourage those behaviours which we consider do not meet these criteria. Through a very simple form of conditioning, the children quickly learn which behaviours meet with adult approval and which do not. They become like us, and the more like us they become, the more we like it and the more approval they get. We are in effect recreating ourselves.

Carl Jung explored the way in which the behaviours which are valued, and therefore which are most often engaged in by the child, go on to form the persona of the child and later adult and become her public image, her concession to the requirements of society. Her persona is an important part of her survival kit, as it helps her to survive as an individual while at the same time satisfying the 'collective' demands of society. The persona is the person's outer psychological mask, made up of all the aspects of herself that she would like society to know about her.

As the child's persona develops through the continued practice of acceptable behaviours, at the same time those behaviours that are not valued are avoided and become part of the child's unconscious. Andrew Samuels' commentary on the work of Carl Jung details how these 'unacceptable behaviours' go to form that aspect of the person which is not visible and which is for the most part repressed or hidden. The aspects of the person which she does not like to acknowledge and which she tries to hide from herself and from others are all consigned to the dumping ground of the unconscious, and go to form the shadow. Though her shadow is unconscious, it is nevertheless a part of the child's psychological makeup and is at all times active and therefore at all times affecting her behaviour, though she is not aware of this.

What this means is that we tend to treat our children as extensions of ourselves and to reward that behaviour which mirrors ourselves, while at the same time extinguishing that behaviour which upsets our view of ourselves. The fact that much of this is an unconscious process and that we as parents are not always aware of what we are doing, does not lessen its impact. It is unavoidable that children will mirror their parents in terms of physique, psychological makeup, emotional needs, responses and even behaviour. The important thing for parents and teachers is to be aware of this, to accept that it happens and that it is necessary for the emotional well-being of both parent and child that this is so.

This sameness provides the young child with the foundation for developing a sense of identity, as well as providing feelings of security and belonging which, as the work of current practitioners such as Tony Humphreys and Denis Lawrence shows, are important as part of the process of building and enhancing self-esteem. It is by becoming consciously aware of these processes that we will be able to make the most important decision of all and acknowledge that our children are not us, they are not extensions of us and do not have the same needs. Nor do they have the same life situations to cotend with and do not need the same skills or capabilities to cope with their life situations. The physical, psychological, emotional and intellectual environment, though similar and close to that of the parents, is at the same time different than that which the parents experienced. The parents will therefore have to make the leap from thinking in terms of what is best for themselves, to what is and will be best for a different person in a different environment. The most effective way of doing this is in being conscious and aware of one's own 'psychological baggage'. All children are more than the sum of their parents' psychologies and physiologies. In addition to the genetic inheritance of their parents' physical, emotional and overall psychological traits, they also inherit to a lesser extent the traits and characteristics of a wider collective, including grandparents and great-grandparents, as well as the environmental influences which have been assimilated by all these people. In addition, the child absorbs her own environmental influences.

And yet the thread running through all this is the parental input. The parents are not only the main contributors to the child's genetic, psychological, emotional and intellectual pool, they are also the primary mediators of society's norms and demands, and as such will act as a filter for the effects of society on the child. What this means is that while there are countless environmental influences on the psyche of the child, all are in one way or another filtered through the parental sieve. This means that all influences, both genetic and environmental, will carry the stamp of the parents' psyche — with all its positive and negative aspects.

As the child grows for the five most formative years of her life in the cocoon of the family home, little or no other outside influence is allowed in. Although more and more children attend pre-schools and nurseries, there is still a strong sense of the sacredness of the family in Irish society, resulting in the fact that the family structure is to all intents and purposes a closed situation. The effect of such closedness can be to create a strong psychological boundary and so give the child a strong sense of who she is, a strong sense of family worth, a strong sense that she is good enough to play a role in the outside world and, most importantly, a strong feeling of being safe. But where the closedness is characterised by secrecy, abuse or fear, it becomes an environment that represses the child's attempts at independence. It has the effect of smothering the child, and produces a child who has no trust in the collective good of society as represented to her by her family.

Robert Reasoner's work on self-esteem provides clear evidence of how important the psychological condition of the family, both collectively and individually, is in the development of the child. The self-image of each family member and the collective self-image of the family as a group, the confidence each family member has in herself and the collective confidence of the family as a group, the belief of each family member to be an effective agent in their own destinies as well as the collective self-belief of the family as a group, all have a bearing on the way in which the child will grow or not grow. Perhaps the most important issue here is the confidence which the child has in her family as a group. All these areas are connected and interrelated in the formation and growth of the child, and serve to illustrate how closely linked the child's world is with that of her parents.

The family with collectively and individually low self-esteem, negative self-image, lack of belief in their own effectiveness and low trust levels, will create an environment in which these negative traits will be seen as desirable, because a confident, assertive child would pose a threat to parents with low self-esteem and negative self-image.

On the other hand, the family that has confidence both in the self and in the 'other' will unconsciously and consciously generate this confidence and reward it in the child who displays it. Hand-in-hand with this is the presence or absence of threat and isolation within the family. Where individuals in a family, and indeed families as a whole, feel that society is not on their side and that they have no say in what goes in society, a negative view of society will be held up for the children. This will lead to mistrust, isolation and an inability to accept authority. The parents' perception of society, whether it accurately reflects society or not, will become the child's, and so will have a major impact on how the child will respond to the outside world when he goes to school. We see from the work of many experts, and in particular from the work of Robert Burns on self-concept formation, how the parents' sense of powerlessness and mistrust will be transmitted to the child as feelings of frustration and apathy. This is both because of their parents' modelling and because of their parents' inability to foster a sense of personal effectiveness.

Many of the problems that arise later in life for both children and adults have their origins in the first years of the child's life and are a reflection of the values and attitudes which underpin the parents' treatment of them. Over-anxiety about the child's welfare when she is born can, as Eric Neumann suggests, lead to the parents not allowing the child any freedom during early and middle childhood, causing the child to be afraid of risks and challenges. Over-concern for appearances and order when the child is young will lead to the child growing up as an adult who is afraid of failure and will lack the 'willingness to try'. Over-concern for the child's safety during the first years of the child's life causes the child to become overly cautious and fearful of other people and any form of uncertainty. The unconscious and unacknowledged issues in the parents become the problems and weaknesses of the children as they grow.

The Effective Child and Difference: The Parents' Role

If as parents we consciously try to take note of the child's differences, and to accept these differences as part of the child's makeup, it will be easier to allow the child to be different. In trying to be aware of, and accepting of, difference in children, it is helpful if we can be aware of our own inner need to make the child like ourselves. We can use this consciousness to develop her separateness.

If the parent can acknowledge her own separateness, and develop a life which is separate from that of the child, it will help in the process of allowing the child to have a life which is outside of the parents' experience and therefore a life which is different. Because of the close physical and emotional protection function of the family in the life of the child, the closeness can often become a form of idealisation, where the life of the parent and the child are so closely connected that there is no sense of separateness. Unconscious unhappiness with her own life may lead to a parent investing her whole life in the life of the child, leading to the child having no separate identity. The most effective way of avoiding this is for the parent to bring to awareness and to confront her own issues about what she wants for herself and what she wants for her children. By ensuring that she has a life that is separate from her children, the parent will realise that there is more to life than her children and be better able to develop difference and separateness in the child.

The process of promoting difference and separateness is helped if parents reward independence and self-reliance. This is a sign to the child that the parents want him to become himself, and it also shows the child that the parents are happy to see him separate. Parents who are willing to give the child the freedom to crawl, to explore, to experiment, to investigate and to take risks, will demonstrate to the child that they are in favour of difference. It will have the dual effect of encouraging the parents to be comfortable with difference, while at the same time giving the child the feeling that it is acceptable to be different.

Children respond to and are reassured by touch. If parents encourage and facilitate lots of physical expressions of affection, it will provide the child with both the emotional and physical confidence in himself to aspire to be different.

One of the ways in which children know that it's OK to be different is when they realise that their parents are around but that they are not in their space. It is often difficult for parents to stay out of their child's affairs, e.g. when the child is having an argument, and they may allow their own unconscious fears about conflict or confrontation to cause them to interfere. If possible, it is more beneficial if parents can stay out of the child's arguments and let her handle them herself.

In accepting the child for who she is, the following guidelines may be helpful:

- Your child is not you!
- If your child is happily playing by herself, do not interrupt just to satisfy your own needs.
- Beware of the 'overs': over-feeding, over-protection, over-valuing, over-clothing.

The Effective Child and Difference: The Teacher's Role

When the teacher is aware of and accepts his own individuality, it will make it easier for him to accept difference in the children. It is helpful that the teacher is aware of his own personality type and the personality type of his colleagues, and that he realises that one type is not superior to another.

Personality type is a process whereby the 'usual way of being' of a person is categorised into one of the two attitudes, extroversion or introversion, and further, into one of the four functions: thinking, feeling, intuition, sensation. Any person has the potential for all these but will typically behave in an extroverted thinking fashion, or an introverted feeling way. It is not a way of labelling the person, but a categorisation of actual and potential ways of behaving.

Where a teacher has become excessively caught up in the collective by being too closely identified with the job of teaching, it makes it difficult for him to see the individual, and there is a tendency to judge everything in terms of group norms. When teachers separate group issues from individual issues, it is much easier to counteract possible identification and to see the child as an individual in the group.

The child's performance is undoubtedly linked to the performance of the teacher, and we can say that the child's success is in some measure a function of teacher effectiveness. However, it is essential that the teacher consciously separates the child's performance from his own sense of worth as a teacher. Put another way, it is reasonable for her and good for the child, if she takes pride in the child's performance, but it is essential that the two are kept separate. If the teacher's professional and personal satisfaction become dependent on the child's performance, it is likely that the child will feel that the teacher's satisfaction and happiness depends on how well she performs in class.

THINGS TO WATCH FOR

- The child who is always imitating others.
- The child who clings to the teacher or parent.
- The child who never seems to have an opinion.
- The child who always asks before doing something.
- The child who is always copying work from another.
- The child who cannot make up her own mind, and repeats what others say.

Andrew's Story

Andrew is a five-year-old, who has just started school. When he started school he was unable to separate from his mother, who also had difficulty separating from her son. Even after a settling-in period, Andrew still showed strong resistance to coming to school. He would cry, complain of tummy-ache, display tantrums and try every way he could think of to make his mother keep him at home. Andrew's mother, in addition to her own anxiety about separating, had to contend with her own guilt at sending Andrew to school.

Sometimes the situation was complicated even further by embarrassment in front of other parents. School was therefore a threatening and unhappy place to Andrew, and he could not understand why his mother would put him into such an inhospitable place each day. Because both parent and child were aware of the other's anxiety without really knowing what was causing it, Andrew's mother tended to project her negative feelings on to the school. This resulted in Andrew picking up the mother's distrust of the school. Andrew's story shows us how, when no separation has taken place, the two identities are still fused together and the mother and child take on the anxiety of the other person.

In school, Andrew retreated into silence because this was the most effective coping mechanism that he had at his disposal. As a result, he did not feel included in the collective life and work of the class. Although this was 'due to his own behaviour', it meant that he was isolated from his peers, and was left behind in the learning which should have provided his daily satisfaction. Gradually he realised that he was excluded and began to resent this, and became aggressive in an attempt to gain entry to the group.

In helping Andrew to come to terms with the separation anxiety, and in helping his mother to allow him to separate and gain confidence in the school, it was important that at no time were either of them made to feel that they were breaking any rules or that they were being punished for wrongdoing. The teacher and the school provided a holding function in which they were able to hold the child both psychologically and emotionally, to facilitate the child's move from mother to school. This is akin to the way in which a mother holds a child and creates a safe space for it. It requires patience and tolerance and the ability to separate the individual needs and feelings of the child from the group norms of the school. The school takes on the role of mother so that the child feels safe in separating from his real mother and moving into the school mother.

CHAPTER 3
TUNING INTO YOUR CHILD

Your child is not you.

Very often the child's needs are confused with the parents' needs. Because a child is a separate person, he will have different needs from other children and from the adults in his life. It is very easy for parents to assume that their child's needs are the same as their own personal needs. Personal needs are based on the individual psychological, social, emotional and physical makeup of the child. His needs are determined by the kind of person he is, what he is capable of becoming, the environment in which he finds himself and his ability or inability to cope with his environment in a way that does not threaten his view of himself. Given the nature of the child–parent relationship it is inevitable that a parent will feel that he 'knows best', and will to some extent be sucked into confusing what are in fact his own needs with the actual needs of the child. Apart from being separate individuals, the children in our care will have to live in, and cope with, a different environment from their parents. The skills which we had when we were children may have been adequate at that time, in that place and for those people, but it is unlikely that the same skills will suffice for a child who is a product of a different environment and who will have to cope with a different set of life situations. A child can only become an effective child if the parents recognise his separate needs.

When the parent, teacher or any other adult projects their own unconscious needs onto the child, the adult believes that their own needs are the same as the needs of the child, and the child in turn believes these to be his own. Projecting adult needs on to the child means that the adult will only be happy if and when the child achieves what the adult wants for herself. These 'adult' needs will be unsuitable for the child. It also means that the child will never achieve his own ambitions. It means that the child is treated as if he 'is' his parents and that the parent sees the child as an extension of himself. It follows that the child will be unable to have a separate identity from the parent. This results in what is termed idealisation, where the child and parent think so highly of each other, that there is a fusion of identities. As a result the child becomes stuck at an infantile stage of emotional development and never manages to separate from the parent, never sees himself as separate and never manages to develop an identity which stands on its own, separate from that of the parent. In practical terms, it means that the child, and later the adult, is unable to make decisions without referring to the parent, cannot form healthy relationships and is always dependent.

We may see this when the child starts school, where for the first time he is taken out of the direct care of the family. There is a certain fear of the unknown effects of 'society' on the child. There is the parental fear, based on unconscious self-doubt, that their child will not be able to cope. This fear is almost entirely based on the parents' own experience of what happened to them when they separated from their parents, and may in part be due to 'incomplete separation' of the parent from his parent. Additionally, there is the assumption by the parents that what happened to them at school will also happen to their children. This can result in the parents resisting the child's separation from them. Even though they allow the child to physically go to school, they find it difficult to allow the child to experience complete psychological and emotional freedom. This full emotional and psychological separation requires trust in the outside world, satisfaction with one's own self-image and confidence in one's own ability to deal with uncertainty, as well as the ability to see and promote these qualities in the child. This psychological and physical separation is made more difficult by the existence of some actual dangers to the child when he starts school. Very often this is the child's first venture outside the protected cocoon of the family, and parents often have difficulties coping with some of the behaviours which the child learns as part of the process of socialisation. This is particularly the case where these new behaviours do not fit into the 'primary family matrix' of behaviour which forms the basis for what is deemed necessary for this family to survive.

The primary family matrix refers to the usually practised forms of behaviour and language which are accepted, valued and encouraged within the family group, and which form the model from which the child learns what is acceptable and desirable for him. Your child is bound to learn new language skills, behaviour patterns and ways of coping with his new environment. In fact, he learns them because he needs them for his own personal survival; when your child comes home from school with a colourful vocabulary, it is an essential part of his learning to be effective in coping with his own life situation as he finds it. It does not mean that the family has to change its values, its attitudes to 'bad' language or that it must unquestioningly accept the child's new coping skills. The primary family matrix of beliefs and behaviour remains an important reference point and base from which the child begins his exploration. The family can and must have confidence in what it believes, for the child to inherit the same confidence in what he believes. But at the same time, the family can have a 'flexible assurance' in itself and in its way of being, so that the child can be a part of and influenced by the notion of confidence in what he is, while at the same time being open to growth and change.

The family system is the way in which all the people in the family fit together and relate to each other, and how well they operate together as a connected whole. It is important for parents to be aware that just as the family system seeks to protect and maintain itself in its own self-view, so also the psyche of each individual within it is also self-regulating and will seek to maintain itself in its own optimal image. What this means is that each child will attempt to follow the path which he considers is the best for him to maintain his own self-view. This process will, as often as not, bring the child into conflict with the group norms of his family. Being aware that this is healthy and normal for a child is important, as it enables the parent to cope with it and not to suppress it. It is healthy for the individual members of a group to test the boundaries and to know that it is allowed as it teaches them the value of challenge, the value of testing limits and the value of doing this within the framework of a secure but flexible boundary. What is meant here by a boundary is the way in which the family, or any group, forms an enclosed psychological and emotional space within which the person feels safe and secure.

The family is the testing ground for the child in his attempts to learn about reality and how best to cope with it. As such, it should provide a realistic representation of what the child will encounter when he leaves the protection of the family boundary. The parents, since they are the grown-ups, the people with experience and the significant adults in the child's life, need to be aware of the fact that when the child flexes his muscles and tests the boundaries of the family, he is engaging in what we call reality testing, a necessary stage in the growth of the child. The ability of the adult to be comfortable with these 'threats' to his self-view and therefore to be able to facilitate the fulfilment of the needs of the child, without feeling that his own survival is being threatened, is of crucial importance to the child's ability to accept authority, deal with conflict and form relationships.

The most effective way to both prevent and counteract the dangers of parent's and children's needs being fused is by tuning into the child.

Parents' natural desire to be in tune with the child often spills over into the realm of interfering unnecessarily in their child's life, and especially interfering in their arguments and fights. This is the adult's unconscious fear of their own inability to cope with conflict; the most serious effect is that it can perpetuate this in the child, by not allowing him to deal with it himself in his own way. It also has the effect of reinforcing the child's dependence on the parent. The willingness to allow the child to do things by himself and to face up to problems without parental interference depends on the parents' confidence in themselves and in the child. The natural instinct in parents to protect their young may become over-active when the child starts school. This over-protection may result in the following:

- The child is not given enough space to grow.
- The child is not allowed to make decisions by himself.
- The child is not allowed to deal with conflict in his own life.
- The child is not allowed to develop confidence in his own judgment.
- The child is prevented from developing a realistic sense of his own capabilities.
- The child is protected from dealing with his own limitations.
- The child may not learn to deal with failure in his life.

Parents and teachers can avoid over-protection, and get closer to the real needs of the child — thus allowing him to become an effective child — if they tune in to the needs and feelings of the child.

Starting school is the first real opportunity that the child has to survive on his own and however much parents consciously say that this is what they want, there is an unconscious need to maintain dependency because it makes parents feel wanted. It is important for both parents to be aware of their own needs, so that the needs of the child can be clear. When the child starts school, his needs may coincide in some degree with the needs of his parents. The child's needs, however, are more likely to centre around needing support (not interference) in his new challenge, needing space to deal with the new social situation and needing his parents to 'hold' his anxiety and sense of achievement, not steal it. It is only by tuning into the child that parents can know what the child's needs are, and so separate their own needs from those of the child.

In learning to tune into your child it is essential to know your own needs, so that you can separate these from the needs of the child. As people involved in the development and shaping of the children in our care, we have to bring into consciousness those needs and desires which often remain unconscious. It is only by so doing that we can avoid the trap of projection, that is, unconsciously assuming that what are really our own needs and faults are the needs and faults of our children.

Secondly, we need to see our children as 'other people', separate from us physically, emotionally and socially. It is an important 'given' that if we are going to tune into the child, we first of all accept that child as being separate and different.

Tuning into the child means doing so at a conscious and at an unconscious level. Tuning in at the conscious level is what we do normally. We listen, watch, observe, touch and generally are aware of the conscious messages being sent by the child and also by being more aware of the conscious messages that we send as parents. What the child says, what he does — laughing, crying, throwing tantrums, his silences, etc. — all tell us something of what is going on in his mind. These may be to some extent the conscious messages that the child sends, but it is the unconscious connection which tells us even more. Observing the child when he is playing on his own and with others, listening to his stories, listening carefully to his questions, taking note of his fantasies and nightmares, all tell us things about the child which he may not be able to tell us.

Above all, if we want to know what the child's needs are we need to give him the space to tell us. Rather than putting pressure on the child to tell us 'what happened', 'why did you do that?', or 'who did that to you?', it is much more informative to allow the child to 'tell his own story'. One of the main dangers of not tuning into your child, at a later stage, is that it leads to the assumption that because as parents we did not get the chance to achieve something — such as go to college — that our children will therefore be best served by going to college. This can result in children doing courses which are more suited to their parents than to the children, being sent to college when in fact they are not suited for it, or being put under pressure to achieve results which are beyond their capability.

Tuning Into Your Child: The Parents' Role

Listening to what the child is saying and to what he has to say is one of the most informative ways of finding out what is important to the child. When the child is speaking directly to a parent, it is sometimes difficult to have the patience and the time to hear him out. If a parent can focus on what the child is saying he will get a lot more from the child. When a child is conversing with another child at play, or especially when he is talking to himself, it gives an insight into the child's mind at any given time.

It is much more inclusive and revealing if adults talk with the child rather than to him. The child feels more connected and valued and will confide more and tell more of what is important to him. When a child is playing, working, sleeping, he is unwittingly telling what is going on for him at that time. It is a help to parents to observe the child, especially if the child is unaware of it, as this tells us the real issues.

Play is the child's expression of his fantasy and represents the child's unconscious expression of his inner thoughts and ideas. If parents play with the child at his own level, and get into the fantasy of his play, they become a part of the child's world, and can tune into what is happening in the child's world.

Circle time device is a way of involving everybody in the group. The whole family sits around in a circle, possibly at the table after a meal. Everyone has a chance to speak and no one interrupts, or laughs. The person whose turn it is to talk has a 'talking stick' or some other tool, which denotes that he has the floor. The main purpose of circle time is to allow every-body to have a say and to enable everyone to be listened to. It helps children to feel included in family business and makes them feel that they belong to the family.

Circle time in a family could work in the following way:

- The family is sitting in a circle, on the floor, at the table.
- Ground rules are agreed by the group together.
- It can be an agreed topic or an open topic.

- The person whose turn it is to talk has a talking stick.
- Everybody in the circle has a 'turn'.
- When a person finishes speaking, she hands the stick to the next person. In this way, the speaker has control over her own contribution.
- 'Turn' means that the person can speak or remain silent if they wish.
- When the circle is complete, there can be a second round, or not, depending on what the 'circle' wishes.

Have a 'no TV day', where the children have time and opportunities to be by themselves, without any technology. This gives the family the chance to develop their own entertainment, and helps to foster communication and conversation. It helps parents to gain insights into their children, by seeing them without the 'shell of technology'.

Every child has dreams, nightmares, day-dreams, fantasies, which are really windows of his mind which allow us to see what are the issues which are causing anxiety, anger or pain. It is important that parents take all these seriously, talk to the child about them and take account of what he is saying.

Allow him the space and freedom to have his own thoughts and ideas. If your child is playing happily by himself, don't butt in. At the same time, encourage and facilitate 'solo' playing.

Don't force him to talk about school, or indeed any aspect of his life, just because you think there is something wrong. If there is something causing the child anxiety it will show, and he will tell you in his own time either unconsciously or consciously. This is the time to observe, listen, talk and play. If the child knows that his parents believe and trust him, he will communicate in a more open and informative way. It is often tempting to check with other children or parents if we suspect that our child has misbehaved. This sends the wrong message to the child, and if the child is given the time and space he will tell you.

Nightmares are very often frightening occurrences and parents can become upset and scared if they see their child having a nightmare. But while overt signs of the nightmare may be frightening, we should really see the nightmare as a symptom of change, or anticipated difficult event in the child's life. It may be a normal change such as learning to walk, to read, etc., which the child is worried that he will not be able to achieve. In other words, it may be 'normal task-oriented anxiety', which we all experience prior to carrying out a new task, or it may indicate something serious in the child's life.

What he needs is reassurance, support and holding. But he does not need the parent to take over and 'solve the problem' for him. It is much more helpful if parents do not confuse their own reaction to the nightmare with what is going on for the child. If parents show fear and anxiety when the child has woken up from a nightmare, it will only add to the child's anxiety. The best thing for parents to do is to be there for the child when he wakes up and to talk about the nightmare, especially if the child remembers any of the details. As an adult you can offer an explanation which will appease the child's fears and possibly lessen the likelihood of a re-occurrence. Parents should avoid the temptation to trivialise the nightmare or to pass it off as a joke, because it makes it easier for the parent to deal with it. It is understandable that a parent who sees her child having a nightmare may become frightened or anxious. If we remember, however, that the nightmare is not of itself harmful, that it is the child's way of telling us that he is growing and that he is reaching a new stage in his development, it will help us to focus on the child's actual need. If it is at a stage when the child is learning to walk, to read, or 'preparing for' some new skill or phase in his life, what he really needs is awareness and support from those around him.

If parents can see the nightmare as an opportunity, because it tells us that there is something in the child's life that he is finding it difficult to cope with, it will be more helpful to the child. The nightmare is his unconscious telling him, and us, that we need to pay attention to this aspect of his life. Anxiety that surfaces during sleep is anxiety which the person either cannot express during consciousness or which he is not aware of. So when the normal defences of conscious living are taken down in sleep, these anxieties are allowed to surface. It is always wise to allow the child the space to talk about his anxieties in his own time and without putting our parental interpretation on his story. In other words, try not to badger the child with questions such as: Is everything all right at school? Is somebody bullying you? Such questions will only put ideas into the child's head. Give him space and support and eventually the problem will manifest by itself.

If your child is unhappy when he is leaving you, for example going to school, going to bed, or when you are going out, this is his way of telling you that there is something 'wrong'. Wait till he is ready to tell you, create a safe space where he can tell you without fear of recrimination. Don't force the issue and don't plant ideas in his head.

Sometimes a child finds it easier to draw a picture of what is wrong than to tell an adult. Then he feels that he is talking about the picture and it is easier for him.

If your child tells a lie about something, it means that he is afraid of something. It may be something he has done that he does not want you to know about, or it may be something which has happened to him and for which he is wrongly blaming himself. But it may also be that he wants to deal with it himself. The important thing is not to force him into a corner in an effort to get at the truth. Telling lies is a sign of fear and if we put pressure on the child to 'tell the truth' we increase the level of fear. In some cases, the child may not be sure what the problem is and may feel under pressure to satisfy the adult and he will simply say what he thinks you want to hear. It is much better to stand back, allow the child some space and let him see that there is a safe space in which he can confide in you. If we adopt an excessively moral approach to the truth, it leads to children not being able to adapt and lacking in initiative. Telling lies is sometimes a necessary assertive response for a child who is under threat and the child needs to know how to do it even if he knows that it is generally not acceptable.

Tuning Into The Child: The Teacher's Role

For the teacher, it is usually a case of getting others to pay attention to what he is saying and getting others to listen. One of the basic prerequisites of the teacher's work is that the children pay attention. This becomes such an important part of the work that listening to what the child is saying may not come easily. Additionally, finding the time and the energy to listen may be difficult. However, if the teacher is to tune into the child and be aware of his needs, then it is essential that he not only listens to what the child is saying verbally, but physically and emotionally as well.

The demands on a teacher's time are neverending and it becomes easy for the teacher to be sucked into a merry-go-round where the emphasis is on getting things done quickly, getting answers immediately and achieving immediate gratification in the scholastic sense. While such an approach can be productive, many children need time to consider what they are going to say and need encouragement and space to say it. In most classrooms, as in society, there are dominant children who always have the answer first and are very assertive about 'getting the teacher to ask them' first. These children may take over the verbal world of the classroom and in so doing push the more passive children into the background. However difficult it is, each child should have the time, the psychological space and the tolerance of both teacher and classmates to say what he wants to say.

If the teacher can observe the child in class and in the playground, it helps him to gain an insight into the child which will help in tuning into his needs.

It is through the child's misbehaviour that the teacher will find out most about the child; if a teacher can look at misbehaviour as a way into the psyche of the child, rather than just something to be eliminated and punished, it can help both teacher and child enormously.

In the same way, the child's moods, tantrums, daydreams and verbal outbursts are windows to the psyche of the child. For a teacher who is under pressure to get the work done, they are most likely to be a nuisance. But if a teacher pays attention to these unconscious messages from the child, he is likely to get closer to the child and to be much more in tune with him.

Using circle time provides the teacher with an opportunity to hear what the child needs to say, and to 'eavesdrop' on the inner thoughts of the children. Circle time also allows the teacher the opportunity to talk with the children as if he were just another member of the group.

In her traditional role as 'superior' and guardian of society's values, there can be pressure on the teacher to 'disbelieve' what the child is saying. Additionally the normal human response of wanting to hide wrongdoing makes it difficult to always believe the child. To gain the child's confidence and to allow the teacher to tune into the child's world, it is helpful if the teacher as a first response takes the child's word seriously and believes until he knows otherwise.

THINGS TO WATCH FOR

- The child who says nothing (he is communicating in other ways).
- The child who is always looking for attention.
- The child who doesn't play.
- The child who never 'steps out of line'.
- The child who does not want to go home.
- The child who finds it difficult to allow others to have their share of the attention.
- The child who is always in a world of his own.

Jean's Story

Jean is twelve, in sixth class, and is the oldest of four children. The family is in transition and there is a sense of insecurity in terms of work, house and relationships. Jean's mother identifies very closely with her and is convinced that the things that happened to her as a child will also happen to her daughter. Jean's father is a strong negative influence in her life, in as much as for the most part he is 'absent' both psychologically and physically. Whatever influence her father tries to exert is resisted by Jean because she resents his mistreatment of her mother, and because she does not trust him. The mother's over-protection and lack of trust in Jean, together with the father's lack of interest — as well as the overall uncertainty in the family — have alienated Jean and caused her to become overly rebellious and aggressive towards her other family members. She uses physical violence and verbal abuse in order to achieve her ends.

Jean's story shows how the dynamics of the relationships within the family system are closely connected and the way in which whatever happens to one member of the family has a bearing on the others, though it may not appear so. It also shows how a relationship that is too close is not a healthy one. Jean is caught in a situation where she has neither a satisfying relationship with her mother or father, nor has she the benefit of being cared for within the boundary of a healthy mother–father relationship. The result is that she is not heard, has no say and feels isolated. She resorts to the most effective and most commonly used method of getting attention in her family, that is aggression, abuse and violence.

Working with Jean was made difficult, as the father was unwilling to become involved; this meant that unless Jean and her mother were able to involve him at some secondary level he would become isolated. In working with Jean, the emphasis was on being heard, having a say and feeling a part of what was going on in the therapy room. This was easy to do in the one-to-one, safe environment of the therapy room, but it was something that was completely new to Jean. Any new skill, whether it is a motor skill or a psychological skill, is difficult for the person to take on and to use, until she gets used to it. Being heard was new to Jean and it took some time for her accept that it was possible to be heard without having to shout. In addition, it was difficult for the mother to accept that she could listen to Jean and not feel threatened.

CHAPTER 4
BELONGING

If we teach them isolation they become disenchanted.

One of the most disturbing failures of modern society is the sense of isolation expressed by young people. It manifests especially in the teenage years and is often cited as a factor in young people taking drugs, committing suicide and other problems which arise in the world of at-risk young people. In developing personal effectiveness and in the development of the person generally, an essential ingredient is that the child feels that she is a part of a greater system: part of a family, part of the school in which she is a pupil, part of the community and part of the country in which she lives. This gives the child the feeling of security by being looked after by something bigger than herself, as well as the feeling of being valued for who she is and what she can contribute. Both school and family have the opportunity to enable the child to feel that she really belongs to the group, that she is valued for who she is in the group, and that she can feel safe within the boundaries of the group.

The child needs to see that there is regular contact between the school and her family to reassure her; she needs to know that her parents trust the school, that the school values the family's involvement in the child's education and that the school welcomes her each day. It is important for the boundaries of the school and the home to be separate and at the same time to overlap, so that the child feels secure and safe in both environments. This enables her to move freely from one safe space to the other without feeling threatened.

It is in feeling that we belong, both as adults and as children, that we gain a sense of security, a sense that we matter and a sense that we are important. It is this feeling of being wanted and accepted by other people, especially those people that we value and those whom we perceive to be powerful, which transmits to the child the sense of her own self-worth. To be effective, the child needs to feel a sense that the other significant people in her life consider her to be effective.

Both at home and in school, the child should be made to feel that she is wanted on the basis of her own personal worth, as a person in her own right. It is this deep inner feeling which the child has that she means something, that she counts for something and that other people value her. In short, it is the feeling that she belongs, which is the key to the child's belief and confidence in herself.

Yet one of the most common sanctions in use in schools and in homes is that of excluding. We suspend children from school, isolate them for misbehaviour, separate them from their peers and send them to their rooms as a means of sanctioning. In examining the effect of such adult behaviour, it is important to be aware of the messages that we as adults send to the children in our care. It is not what we intend to convey, or what we would like to convey, that is important. It is what it means to the child that is important. Very often the signals that we intend to transmit to the child are not the messages she receives. So when we send a child to her room, put her outside the classroom door or suspend her from school, we may intend to say to her that what she has done is not acceptable. Our intention may be to remind the child of her misbehaviour and to prevent it happening again.

By separating the child and putting her outside the boundary of the family, class or the school, however, we are saying to her that she only belongs to the group when she behaves in a certain way. The emotional message is one of rejection and iso-lation, from which the child learns two things: (1) If she wants to 'get away' from authority she can easily do it by repeating the behaviour; (2) Society deals with problems by isolation and rejection rather than by inclusion and negotiation. It is a form of 'conditional acceptance' which convinces the child that isolation and exclusion are acceptable forms of behaviour.

By excluding a child, even though we may have what seems like a very good reason, we are in essence saying 'we don't want you to be part of this group', 'you are not wanted or needed', 'you do not belong'. We are further saying that the best way to deal with this problem is by pretending that it has nothing to do with this group and that we don't want to know about it. We are also saying 'I really can't deal with this situation and I would rather hide it away somewhere where it can't be seen and where it won't bother me'. So we are showing the child a model of personal ineffectiveness rather than modelling an 'I can do it' approach to life.

Effective groups make effective people and effective people make effective groups. If an individual is causing problems in a group then the solution should be related to the group. If an individual is 'damaging' the integrity of the group, then the group is as much at fault as the individual. As long as the individual is a problem, or absent, then the group remains dysfunctional. It is only when the individual is reintegrated into the group that both individual and group can be seen as healthy.

The pressure on teachers or parents to take action in the short term to alleviate a situation, to do something that will allow them to get on with the work in the interests of the majority, is easily understood. This is usually the conscious reason why pupils are suspended or isolated. In the context of the family, when a parent has reached her limit in terms of being able to cope with tantrums etc., it is easy to see why sending the child away is an attractive option. Likewise in the school situation, it is understandable that where a child is being particularly disruptive, the teacher will seek a short-term solution.

But whatever our conscious motivation, or whatever our intention as parents and teachers, when we separate, isolate or suspend a child, it is very probable that the message to the child is one of rejection and isolation. It usually leads to simmering resentment and anger, with no communication, no discussion and no negotiation. The idea is formed in the child's mind that this is the correct way to handle conflict and disagreement, and it leads to sullenness and silence, loneliness and isolation. As well as causing the child to feel left out of the group, that she doesn't belong, it generates feelings of aloofness. It teaches that problems are 'solved' by avoidance rather than by engagement, by isolation rather than by inclusion and by silence rather than by negotiation and discussion.

Belonging and the Effective Child: The Parents' Role

It is a useful to have regular family talks. This will help the child and the parents to feel a sense of collective responsibility, and a part of the decision-making process. As well as fostering a sense of belonging in the family group, this will encourage responsibility and decision making.

When your child misbehaves, try not to use exclusion as a sanction. It is much more valuable and lasting to keep the child within the safe boundary of the family while dealing with the problem.

Some children in a family will be better able than others to get involved in the goings-on in the family. If parents are conscious of this, they will be better able to ensure that all the children are involved in what happens in the family. Where a family member, either child or adult is involved in 'success' or 'failure', allow all the family to share in this. It is possible to share success without stealing the thunder of the child and also to share the 'bad bits' without making a child feel guilty. This is a way of fostering collective responsibility and 'other awareness'.

It is important to be aware of the use of the word 'blame'; 'responsibility' is a more valuable word because it has a positive ring to it and does not have the negative emotional baggage that seems to go hand-in-hand with the word 'guilt'. In the normal everyday activities of the family, this means attributing responsibility where it is warranted, whether it is negative or positive responsibility. It allows the child to accept responsibility for either the positive or negative behaviour, and therefore to own it. It helps the child to learn acceptance of his positive and negative aspects, and not to want to hide them.

Try to be aware whether your children are introverts or extroverts. An introvert is a person who is quiet, thoughtful and enjoys solitude and privacy. It is not the same thing as being shy and is in no sense abnormal. A person who is introverted is more interested in ideas and inner things than in outside events and people. An extrovert, on the other hand, is a child who likes the company of other children, is happy to express himself openly and is at ease in a group. Introverts are more prone to remain on the margins and to become aloof, and may need a little more help to share, to join in and to participate in group activities.

Extroverts are more at ease with other people and find it easier to join in and to be a part of what is going on. Introversion and extroversion are not in any sense 'wrong' and parents should not try to change a child who is introverted. Sometimes we may as parents feel under pressure from other parents and from professionals to encourage our child, who may be introverted, to become outgoing and extroverted. If your child is generally happy within himself allow him to be so. In other words, if it's not broken don't fix it.

Encourage and allow space for your children to share. Sharing has to do with space, time, food, feelings and objects. The ability to share is learned by seeing others doing it and by being able to trust and to accept other people's needs as legitimate. Feeling and knowing that a particular toy is 'mine' is of course a necessary part of psychological well-being; but an unhealthy attachment to either objects or people is telling us that our child may not be secure enough in himself to trust other children.

Your child needs to belong to other groups that are outside the immediate sphere of influence of the family or the school. The child will sense whether we are in favour of this or not; an easy way to encourage and facilitate this type of belonging is to give children the opportunity to walk to school together. This may seem like an unacceptable level of risk, but if it is at all possible, going to school in groups, away from the discipline and supervision of adults, affords the children the space and freedom to interact, socialise, swap stories and generally belong to a group which is not adult oriented.

Separate bedrooms are probably a recent phenomenon and a sign of our prosperity and as such have many merits. However, this can deprive children of opportunities to chat, talk and to have fun away from the supervision but under the protection of the family. Bedtime is a time for gradually winding down and for getting ready to go to another world. While children need to know that their parents or guardians are present, sharing bedrooms can give them the chance to belong to a sub-group within the family, a group which will also provide them with increasing security as they grow.

It is often tempting to get involved in children's disagreements and arguments, because of our own fears and experiences. This may be an unconscious reaction on the part of the parent or teacher; the signal to the child may be that 'Mammy/daddy thinks I can't handle this'. If we can allow the child to deal with his/her own disputes, it is a vote of confidence in the child's ability, as well as an opportunity to develop the skill of negotiation.

Always believe what your child tells you, at least until you know otherwise. If you find that your child has not told you the truth, there is a reason for this and he needs to know that you can accept the real story. He will learn this when he finds out that you know and by your reaction.

Try to see the child's behaviour as separate from the child. Of course, the child must take responsibility for his behaviour. If you feel that it is necessary to punish or sanction, it is better for the child and for your relationship with him if he realises it is the behaviour which is unacceptable and not the child himself.

Belonging and the Effective Child: The Teacher's Role

Circle time is a very inclusive mechanism for showing children and adults that they belong and that they are valued by their peers as well as by their class and school.

In a situation where a child's behaviour is interfering with the welfare of other children, it is often tempting to isolate the child, or put him sitting by himself. But if this is our response, it may become the child's way of achieving in front of his peers, and it may act as a positive reinforcement and encourage the child to repeat the behaviour. It will also reinforce the idea that the child is not a part of the group. The other children will soon pick up what is happening and the child will be labelled as 'bold'.

During PE, there is often a tendency to play elimination or knockout games where the last person in is the winner. It can be helpful in the process of making the child feel part of the group and giving him a sense of belonging if we encourage a more participatory approach to sport, where the emphasis is on cooperation and involvement rather than competition and exclusion.

If we wish to make the child feel that he belongs to the school and that he has a personal space within the emotional environment of the school, we can show this by providing a welcoming and open environment to the school. We can do this by implementing a number of quite simple and easy to practise strategies:

- Have a school policy that all teachers refer to children by christian names rather than surnames.
- Get to know as many children by name as you can.
- Try to have a teacher at the door to welcome the children in the morning.
- Take the time to talk informally to children.

THINGS TO WATCH FOR

Introversion is not something we should try to change. It is not a 'fault', but the introverted child is more prone to remain on the fringes and to become aloof. She is particularly at risk if she is isolated or excluded. She will therefore need to be watched for signs of marginalisation and aloofness. Introversion has to be accepted by the parents and by the teacher, and the child has to know that it is just an aspect of difference, like tallness or hair colour. An introverted person will not be as assertive as an extroverted child, and there is nothing to be gained by constantly pressuring her to be more outgoing or pushy. This will only serve to draw attention to the fact that she is different and to reinforce the idea in the child's mind that in some way she is inferior to her peers. So it is important to allow her to be introverted and quiet, if that is her type, and to accept this and to make sure that she knows that she is accepted.

Watch out for the child who prefers to play on the fringes of games and who seems not to want to get involved. Again, the answer is not to force the issue either by making the group accept her or by forcing her to join the group, as both of these are artificial and do not address the problem. It is much more effective to work with the child and accept her as a member of the class, school or school team and at the same time help her to become more sure of herself.

Watch for children who try to disrupt other children's games. This is usually a sign that they are being excluded by the other children (perhaps for a valid reason in the children's world) and it is the child's 'legitimate' reaction to being excluded and is in fact her way of trying to gain access to the group. In most cases, it is better to allow the children to sort this out themselves, but it may become useful to have a circle time about it or for the teacher/parent to intervene with the children as a group.

Children isolating peers because of a physical, learning or other disability can happen as a result of a child attending a specialist teacher in the school, as a result of bullying, or as a result of a careless comment by a parent or a teacher. In addition, it may be due to some physical or psychological trait that the child has. Much of this behaviour, sometimes referred to as bullying, is to a large extent unconscious for the children. They do know what they are doing, but they are not aware of the underlying dynamics. So what is required is a group session with the children to bring all the implications and the feelings to the surface and make them aware of all aspects of their behaviour.

Pat's Story

Pat went to school at five. His mother reported extreme behavioural difficulties with him at home, and felt it would be very difficult for the school to cope with his needs. It was clear that there were severe learning difficulties as well. Pat was unable to sit at his place for even the shortest span of time, he was unable to play with other children, and had none of the skills which are normally associated with children starting school, such as sharing attention, other awareness, sharing space, or the ability to defer gratification. When he wanted his own way, or when he did not want to do 'what he was told', he had a number of very effective defences. He would either become extremely violent toward his teacher or the other children, throw furniture, run away or physically and psychologically freeze, so that everybody and everything was shut out.

In the playground he would try to join in with other children, but this would last only for a very short time; as soon as he encountered any difficulty he would run away.

The key with Pat was to let him see that no matter how serious or antisocial his behaviour was, he was still accepted and wanted. In the beginning, his school day was shortened to help both the child and his teacher. This had mixed results. It was also agreed that all the teachers and ancillary staff had an involvement with Pat and that he was not just the responsibility of his own teacher. This meant that Pat could connect with any adult in the school, and feel that he was part of a greater system, which cared for him. In treating Pat's behaviour as unacceptable, while accepting Pat himself, we had to be sure that he was aware of his own responsibility for his behaviour and that this behaviour was not acceptable. The shortened day was helpful, as the physical demands on Pat were such that he needed rest. In another way, the shortened day was sending the wrong message to Pat and to the other children. It was creating the impression that he did not belong with the other children. By agreement with his parents and teacher, all formal learning demands were postponed until Pat was 'ready'.

CHAPTER 5
SEPARATION AND ATTACHMENT

Attachment to parents: umbilical bunjee jumping

From the moment of a child's birth, his life is a continuous process of separation and attachment. Birth itself is a deep, and traumatic separation and the essence of a person's life is a continuous process of balancing the child's attempts at autonomy and independence against the attachment which she feels for the parent, and which the parent feels for the child.

Separation and attachment go hand-in-hand and the effective child is one who can experience both without damaging effects. The parents play the most significant role in the continuous dynamic of separation and attachment, though it involves all the people involved in the child's life. When we talk of separation, it is not just the physical separation of the child from the parent. Associated with separation of parent and child is a very strong emotional memory which reminds the child of all the separations he has had, which brings with it a fear that he may have of extreme separation or abandonment. Though the child may not have been consciously abandoned in the 'actual' sense of the word, he is emotionally connected at an unconscious level with the times when his parents were separated from him through hospitalisation, holidays, or for other extended periods.

It is not necessary to address this issue with the child, as he is probably not aware of it; in any case, it is through normal everyday living that it is best addressed. It is by keeping the child informed when we have to go out, telling him when we will be back and generally including him in discussions about where we are going. The child very quickly learns that we will be back when we say we will, that we mean what we say and that we can be trusted.

By far the most important aspect of this process is the mother's ability to let go. During pregnancy, there is complete fusion psychologically and physically between mother and child. Whatever happens to the mother also happens to the child. Although the father is not physically attached at this stage, he has a role to play in as much as his presence, absence, support or opposition will have an effect on the psychological well-being of the mother, which is transmitted to the child. This psychological fusion of mother and child gives a unique and lasting character to the mother–child relationship. It means that for the mother there will be not only an emotional but also a physical separation. Though the physical separation occurs at birth, it is not until later in the first year of the child's life that the child begins to see the mother as a separate entity. This is not to say that complete psychological separation occurs at this point, and indeed it may be true to say that complete and total psychological and emotional independence is never really complete.

In other words, there is always some element of emotional dependence between parents and children. It works both ways. Parents are emotionally dependent on their children and the children are emotionally dependent on their parents. Complete separation and independence would mean isolation and loneliness. The issue here is to achieve a good working balance between allowing the child to become emotionally independent while at the same time maintaining a holding, supporting presence at a distance that is close enough for the child to know it is there, but not so close that it smothers the child's emotional development. The effective child is one who can get on with his life whether his parents are there or not.

Separation and attachment are important factors in the father-child relationship also. In the Nineties, the most noticeable factor in this is the absent father. He can be physically absent through marriage break-up, work or addiction, or he may be physically present but emotionally absent. The absent father means that the child has no masculine role model, no father figure and masculine model of legitimate power in his life. This can engender feelings of powerlessness in the child, feelings of guilt at what the child may see as his fault, or an overemphasis on the feminine. It can cause the child to develop an ambivalent attitude to authority. Where the father is present in a 'good enough' capacity the child will develop healthy attitudes to authority, a legitimate sense of his own power and a realistic and balanced sense of his own gender.

Linked into this is the father's ability and willingness to let the child go. Consciously, a father can say that he wants his child to be independent of him, but through his own unconscious fears for the safety of the child, mainly rooted in his own lack of trust and confidence in others, he may be unconsciously inhibiting the child's attempts at independence. To make this more difficult, there is also the danger that the child may be abandoned by the father, in which case the child suffers from feelings of guilt and rejection. Abandonment fears may be caused by an addiction to work, to sport or recreation, or to alcohol, or by marital separation. An absent father is simply a father who is not present for prolonged periods of the child's day, especially at those times when the child is going from one aspect of his day to another, such as going to school, going to bed, when he wakes up, or when he is having meals.

The modern phenomenon of the working mother, the childminder and going to playschool, coming as they do early in the life of the child, all have the effect of causing anxiety for the child as well as guilt for the mother. These minor transitions may appear to adults to be inconsequential and insignificant, but to the child they are transitions, and therefore involve feelings of insecurity and anxiety. It is at these times that parents are needed to facilitate and ease the transition and to reassure the child that he has the capability to do it and that there is help and support if he needs it.

These minor transitions serve as models for the major transitions in a person's life, and the way in which the minor ones are dealt with will affect the way in which the major transitions are handled. The major transitions are: being born, starting school, starting secondary school, leaving home for college and getting married. These are the major 'external' transitions; there are also internal transitions which are not as noticeable, but which are just as important and influential. These are the transitions from complete psychological and physical fusion with the mother to physical and psychological birth, from infancy to early childhood, from early to middle childhood, the transition to adolescence and the transition to adulthood. All transitions, provided they are monitored, are marked by a lessening of the attachment to the mother and father and at the same time an increase in the child's ability to 'fend for himself' both physically and psychologically. The effective child will be able to negotiate these transitions because he feels secure in the knowledge that he has support, if he needs it.

All the transitions, while not always marked by overt physical symptoms and therefore not always evident, are nonetheless an influential part of the ongoing life pattern of the child. It is at these times that the child's anxiety levels increase and his need for nurture and holding is greater. It is by tuning into our child that we will know when to hold and when to hold back. The minor transitions are indicators to the child of the level of commitment of the adults around him, and they will either give him confidence in addressing the major transitions, or they will make him feel that he is on his own. But it is balance that is required. The parents who crowd the child and who don't allow him space in making these transitions will do just as much damage as the parents who are not present at all. What is required at times of transition is a sympathetic, supportive presence, rather than a smothering presence or an undermining absence. The effective child is one who has become psychologically and emotionally adept at negotiating these major and minor transitions.

There is strong evidence to suggest that psychological birth or complete separation from the mother does not occur for about one year after physical birth, and that for the first year of the child's life he sees himself and his mother as one person. It is even more than this. The child sees the mother as a part of him, and when the mother is absent the child feels that he himself is under threat and in danger of annihilation.

If the trauma of physical birth is considered critical in the child's experience, then it must also be that psychological birth has the same level of effect on the child. The way parents handle separation depends very much on how they feel about themselves. During the first year of the child's life, what he needs is an encompassing protective space inhabited by himself and his parents. Even at this early stage the child is aware of presence and absence, aware of love or unlove, aware of nurture or neglect. Although he is not able to articulate his needs verbally, he knows what is happening to him and is communicating this to his parents in ways which may not be immediately understandable to the parents. Hence the need to tune in to the child.

During the child's pre-school years the extent to which he is allowed to do things for himself, to explore and take risks, and the attitude of his parents to this type of freedom, sets the tone and the scope of the child's confidence and achievement levels for the rest of his life. Being encouraged to explore, to play, to be inquisitive and to find out, while at the same time feeling the nurturant safety net of his parents, teaches him that he not only has the ability to do, but that he also has his parents' support and the freedom to follow his intuition. These are lessons which will stay with him during his life.

Separation, Attachment and the Effective Child: The Parents' Role

It is a natural instinct and an intrinsic part of the learning process that a child likes to explore his environment. This means his physical and emotional environment, as well as his intellectual and social environment. It is also understandable that as the people responsible for the young child's safety, we may seek to curb this desire for exploration. In trying to help our children to become effective, we should try to be conscious of the ways in which our protective instincts may sometimes interfere with the child's attempts to explore. By allowing and encouraging exploration, we are giving the child the chance to experience new things and at the same time showing him that we have faith in him to take on new challenges. Separation is a normal process in the growth of the child and we should not be afraid to allow the child to experience the sadness of separation. If we want the child to be able to handle separation and to make his own way in life, then he must be exposed to the reality of separation. Our role as parents is to hold and support, not to deprive the child of experiences that we may remember as having being painful for ourselves.

Separation anxiety is the term used to describe the feelings of anxiety that accompany any separation from a loved one, especially if the person is unsure about the separation. It is experienced by both children and adults and its symptoms may manifest as physical pain whose cause the person is unaware of. Both children and parents will experience separation anxiety to some degree when the child starts school. If parents are aware of this and allow the child to express his feelings about it, while at the same time 'holding' the child's anxiety, it will enable the child to cope with the separation in an effective way. We should be aware that separation anxiety is not always a problem, and that most people deal with it and are not adversely affected by it.

In creating a place where the child can develop personal effectiveness, the child will respond to being allowed to make her own decisions, in an atmosphere of support and non-judgment. The 'permission' to make a decision is taken by the child to be a vote of confidence by the parents in her ability, and a vote of confidence in the child's move to separate from her parents. The fear for parents is that the child may not be able to do it or that she will make the wrong decision, and we very easily communicate this fear to the child without realising what we are doing.

If we allow the child to look after herself and her own possessions as much as possible, we are not only saying to the child 'I think you can do this', we are also saying 'I want you to do this', and the unconscious message to the child is 'I am happy for you to be different and separate from me'. Apart from the practical advantage of teaching the child personal competence, we are showing the child how to value and accept difference. Most importantly of all, we are enabling the child to begin the process of separation in a safe, supportive place.

If we have a tendency to be over-concerned with order and neatness, it is possible that we stifle creativity and independence. Excessive order and neatness are really ways of controlling those around us and if a child is caught up in a family system which is very controlling, it will influence his separation from parents by making him feel that it is 'not a good thing' for him to do. In practical terms for parents, this means not being over-fussy about objects in the house; not being upset if the child's room is untidy; not becoming angry or worried when the child makes a mess or a mistake.

It is also helpful to the child's ability to separate if we are open and honest about what we are doing, where we are going and when we will be back. It is often easier to 'tell lies' to a child just to enable you to get away without a fuss. When your child is starting school, it may seem easier to pretend that you are not leaving him or that you will be back in a few minutes, because it gets you out of an embarrassing situation. If parents can be aware of their own needs in this situation, and of the possibility of projecting their own separation anxiety onto the child, it will help the child to separate without too much anxiety. By keeping our promises and not making promises which we can't keep, we are providing the child with a solid base of trust and openness which is a signal to him that you trust him and that you know he is able to be separate and be himself.

Separation and Attachment: The Teacher's Role

Separation anxiety is a normal part of starting school and it is better for the child if we accept this. If we allow our own fears or embarrassment to dominate, it is likely that we will convince the child that it is wrong for him to cry when he misses his mother.

There is a temptation to trivialise separation anxiety by dismissing it as parent/child tantrums, because this makes it easier for us to maintain our status as the professional in the situation. There is the added pressure for the teacher to 'get on with the work', and we may find that it is difficult to have the time for what we see as non-school issues.

Allow the child/parent to express their feelings about their separation, and if a child or parent is upset by the separation of starting school, allow them some time and space together in a quiet part of the school.

It is important for the child to know the truth about the parent being at home and when he will be in to collect the child.

Allow parents into the classroom so they can be reassured. If the parent knows what the classroom is like and what the teacher is like, he will have more confidence in the school and will be happier to leave his child there.

THINGS TO WATCH FOR

- Allowing our own fears to limit what we allow the child to do.
- Projecting our own fears on to the child. In other words, thinking that because we are afraid of something that the child will also be afraid.
- Overprotecting. If the child doesn't have the opportunity to deal with situations, he will not acquire the skills needed to deal with them in later life.
- 'Doing it for the child' rather than with the child.
- The child who can't finish things because of over-attention to neatness and order.

- The child who cannot be away from parents.
- The child who does not settle in school.

Barry's Story

Barry was a seven-year-old boy who came to see me because he was being bullied in school and at play at home. He presented as a very intellectually bright but timid boy, who was reluctant to allow his mother to leave him in the therapy room. The bullying was in the main verbal and Barry was unable to cope when other children called him names which he considered to be 'bad' words. It was clear that the problem lay more in the emotional connotations/attachments of the words which the children were using than in the aggressive behaviour. Barry had an excessively moralistic reaction to the 'names' he was being called, a reaction that was encased in emotional baggage from his parents. Put another way, Barry found the 'bad' words so upsetting that he could not cope, became emotionally distressed, was unable to do his work, and usually ran 'to mammy' for help. It is also significant that it was to his mother that he turned, which suggested that the problem was in some way connected with his relationship with his mother.

In helping Barry to deal with what was causing him to be upset and distressed, it was necessary to give him the tools for coping. It would have been helpful if the 'others' involved could have been involved in the process of dealing with the problem, but this was not possible, so it was necessary to equip Barry to deal with it himself. The tools for coping in Barry's case were both emotional and verbal. It was necessary to detoxify and disempower the 'bad' words which Barry was afraid of, and at the same time provide him with the skill and the vocabulary to 'stand up for himself verbally', whenever it was necessary.

When Barry began to learn the tools for coping, i.e. the language that was necessary to cope with his own distress, but which his parents found distasteful, it was noticeable that a distance began to appear between him and his mother. This was in fact part of the process of psychological separation that was necessary for Barry to develop his own identity and to learn both the need and the skill of 'standing up for himself'.

CHAPTER 6
AUTONOMY AND CONTROL: BOUNDARY AND SPACE

*The freedom to grow requires the
protection of society.*

A child needs space to grow and a boundary to protect this growth. Achieving the correct balance for your child between freedom and control has life-long effects. Too much freedom of choice can be interpreted by the child as uncaring neglect on the part of the parents, and can result in the child learning that her life's decisions can be made without reference to the outside world, without taking into account those around her. It gives the child an unrealistic view of herself and others, and results in an adult who has difficulties relating on an equal basis to the people around her. It makes children into bullies or overly passive adults, both of whom are unable to form equal relationships with those around them.

On the other hand, too much control stifles the child. It prevents her from making decisions on her own, learning what she is capable of and ultimately makes her over-dependent on people who will not always be there. Over-control causes both the child and the adult to believe that the child cannot do things for herself and this notion becomes an accepted part of the psychological map of the family unit. It is this combination of over-dependence and lack of awareness of her capabilities which is most damaging to a child. Over-dependence on others means that in any situation where she has to decide, choose, or solve a problem, she will not have had enough practice in choosing or acting on her own judgment. Nor will she have the confidence in her own ability to choose, so she will be more susceptible to bullying and to being dominated by others. In this she is then conceding control to the other people in her environment and of course losing the chance to have a say in her own life. The effective child is one who has experienced both freedom of choice and parental guidance in reasonable amounts and who has the confidence of others in her ability to choose, to make decisions and to solve problems.

To become good at something we must practise it whether it is a physical, a social or an emotional skill. If we don't get the opportunity to practise, we will not be able to develop the skill, nor have the competence or confidence to use it when the need arises. Too much freedom, or too much control, denies the child the opportunity to practise the social, emotional and physical skills which are integral to the effective child.

For the very young child, the boundary provided by the family circle is her guarantee of safety, her ring of confidence, her extra-uterine reminder of the security she had in the womb. If this boundary becomes broken — perhaps through hospitalisation of mother or child, or through abandonment — then the child's space is contaminated and she feels threatened by fears of destruction. It is the parents, in particular the mother, who forms the boundary; and within this family circle the facilitating environment for the child's growth is held. The boundary can be broken where the mother fails to perform the holding function to reassure the child in the face of impending anxiety. It can also be damaged where the father fails to give the mother the protection and support she needs to enable her to give the child the support *he* needs. And of course it is damaged where either father or mother is absent, or where confidence and trust in adults is broken through violence or neglect.

Where the boundary is broken or damaged through absence, the child's growth is interrupted, or even halted, and the difficulty of restarting the process is greater because of the anxiety that the child associates with the failure of the system. Where separation has occurred for a prolonged period through, for example, hospitalisation, school, parental separation or bereavement, it is often necessary to begin back at the point where the separation occurred, because the child's emotional development may have become stuck at this point. It is damaging to skip over any part of a child's growth, such as happens when a child is pushed too hard, or when he starts school before he is ready. This damage can only be remedied by allowing the child to go back to the point where the damage to his boundaries occurred. The child's development is not something which can be put together piecemeal like a jigsaw. Each stage has its place, not only in the spatial and time senses, but also in the emotional sense; and each succeeding stage depends for its success on the success of the stage which goes before.

When a child is traumatised, her emotional development will be interrupted and her psyche will put it on hold until it is ready to continue. As parents and teachers, we need to be in tune with this, and be able to wait until the child is ready to continue. This can be very difficult for adults, as society tends to demand standardisation in everything. If our best friend's child is able to socialise and mix at a certain age, we tend to demand that our own child should also be able to. Where the child is abandoned or severely neglected, there is no secure boundary for the child and she feels intense anxiety and worry about her safety. Where parents give the child total freedom to choose, in the mistaken belief that this will make her more popular with other children, or indeed because it is too much trouble to care for the child, they will find that this freedom has the same effect as broken, damaged or no boundaries and causes anxiety for the child. It has the additional effect of driving the child to seek a secure boundary elsewhere, often leading to children seeking identification and approval from 'non-legitimate' role models in the community.

In the process of making our children effective in their own lives and environment, the question of power and control is important. The effective child has control over her own world and at the same time does not resent reasonable control and authority. It is in the very first years of the child's life that she learns the 'power of power'. It is our approach as parents to power and autonomy which teaches the child how to use power. It is from the parent that she learns the need for power, the value of power and 'how to use it'. If the parent keeps too tight a rein, gives the child no say in his life and dictates to the child, then the child learns this model of using power. Even though she is at the receiving end of the process, she will quickly learn how to survive in it and will become more at home in the role of passive acceptance. At the same time, she will see that it is the person with the power who has the control and will try to emulate this way of behaving. Where, however, the child experiences no control, and has total freedom to do as she pleases, she never learns how to compromise and never develops the 'other awareness' which is necessary for all relationships. Total freedom is in reality an abdication of responsibility and care, and the child experiences it as an emotional wilderness where there is no sense of having a secure boundary.

The balance that is required to enable children to be effective is one where there is control and autonomy hand-in-hand, where there is boundary and space hand-in-hand, and where there is mutual recognition of the other.

Control and the Effective Child: The Parents' Role

One of the most challenging tasks for parents is to be able to identify their own fears and to separate them from what their children's fears may be. Because of the parents' protective role in the children's lives, they may assume that the things which were a problem for them as children will also be a problem for their children. If parents can become aware of their own unconscious fears and issues, they will be better able to identify the real fears of the child and therefore to deal with them.

To help the child to grow as a healthy individual, it is helpful if there is space within the safe boundary of the family. The child needs the security and safety of a complete boundary, but at the same time he needs his own space within that boundary. This tells the child that you have faith in him as a separate person, while at the same time allowing him the safety of the group. Your child needs a secure physical, emotional and social boundary within which he has emotional, physical and intellectual space.

Children are more influenced by what is done to them and with them than by what is said to them. In trying to foster ideas of control, autonomy and effectiveness in children, the most significant factor is the model of these ideas that we present to our children in the normal way of being which is our everyday life at home. If we wish our children to be able to control their lives, then we must allow them to have control, by respecting their decisions, by not being over-critical when wrong decisions are made and by creating an atmosphere in which personal decision-making is acceptable.

One of the most difficult 'skills' for a parent to develop is the ability to stand back. Children naturally look for help and support when they are in trouble, and the more we intervene and help our children, the more they will seek our help. Asking for help is both a natural instinct and a developed habit. If we help a child every time we think he needs help, he will develop the habit of learned helplessness, and the child will not learn to take control of his own life. It is often more helpful to a child if we do not help, but we allow the child to help himself. This means standing back at times when we may not find it easy to do so. Giving help to another more vulnerable person is a way of satisfying unconscious need for power; it is helpful for adults to be aware that in doing something for a child, we may be satisfying our own power needs rather than empowering the child.

In trying to model individual effectiveness within the boundary of a group, the way in which we deal with dominance and equality will become the way in which the child deals with integration and partnership in his own life. It is helpful to the whole family dynamics and to the child's personal effectiveness, if the parents are aware of tendencies towards dominance or favouritism among their children. If the model is tolerant and accepting of all the members of the family, then this is the way of being which the child will adopt. But if the model is authoritarian and unquestioning then this is the approach that the child will adopt.

We can help the child to use control in a healthy and non-threatening way by:

- Encouraging questions.
- Answering questions.
- Giving your child a say.
- Including the child in family decisions.
- Allowing the child to carry out tasks on his own.
- Encouraging their child to show initiative.
- Hearing the child's side of the story.

- Creating a climate in the house where people take responsibility for what they say and do.

Control and the Effective Child: The Teacher's Role

The classroom and the school are also models of control for the child. The way in which the adults in the system deal with issues of control, freedom and autonomy serve as guidelines for the children in their own lives. It is to this model that they will revert when they leave the school environment.

The traditional view of the teacher as being in total control of the class and therefore the sole decision-maker, meant that the child perhaps did not have a say in his life at school, and would send messages of 'top down' control rather than involvement and consultation. Allowing the child to have a say in the business of the classroom teaches him that consultation works. It also shows the child that he has the ability to be part of a decision-making process.

If we use circle time as a means of including children in the emotional space of the group, it will help not only their sense of belonging but also their ability to contribute in a group situation.

A classroom situation very closely mirrors what happens in society as a whole and we need to be aware of the possibility for dominant children to impose themselves and to take over. The very bright, assertive, articulate child can easily become the 'star' of the classroom and he can unconsciously take over the emotional space that is meant to be shared. This gives the child an unhealthy amount of control and teaches the other less assertive children an hierarchical view of control.

If we become too immersed in our roles as teachers, we can reinforce the idea in the child's mind that might is right,

and will provide a model for the child of dominance, author-
itarianism and self-righteousness. We need to be able to
suspend our own dependence on our superiority as people
and our status as teachers as way of surviving in the classroom, and at particular times to be able to be on equal terms
with the children we teach. We have enormous power in our
classrooms and it is extremely important that we are aware of
the possibilities for unconsciously misusing this power.

The way in which a teacher conducts business in the
classroom becomes a model for the children's own lives. If the
ethos of the classroom is tolerant and accepting rather than
authoritarian and unquestioning, then the children will model
their own lives on the tolerant/accepting model. Children
become what is done to them.

We can help the child to understand and use power effectively and positively by:

- Encouraging an open rather than a closed system in the
  classroom.
- Trying to take account of the children's opinions.
- Consciously trying to include the child who seems to prefer the margins.
- Watching for the 'star' and the 'scapegoat' in the class.
- Ensuring that the passive, quiet or shy child gets time and
  space to make his contribution.
- Being aware of the excessive attention seeker. All children
  and all people seek attention at times, but where a child is
  attempting to monopolise the teacher's attention because he
  is unable to share it, it is important to note this and to try
  to find out why.

Mary's Story

Mary is a woman in her forties who is married and had four children. She was brought to see me by her sister, because she was unable to come by herself. When she came into my room, she looked 'beaten', and her whole behaviour was of a person who had given up.

Mary had been married for more than twenty years, and for the duration of her marriage she had been abused by her husband. The abuse was entirely verbal, but because of her upbringing, her religious beliefs and her inherited view of 'the place of the woman', she had been unable to name the behaviour of her husband and therefore unable to deal with it. Mary's weak point was that she couldn't 'stand' bad language, and it was on this that her husband focused, using it to bully and to control her. He used words such as, bitch, whore, bastard, etc. These words had such an effect on her that she became so upset that she became powerless, unable to respond. She began to blame herself for her inability to have a proper marriage and a happy family. Her situation was made more difficult because of her loyalty to the children. She had reached a point where she was unable to cope and felt there was no reason to live.

For a number of sessions, Mary was unable to do more than cry, and it was extremely difficult for her because she felt guilty about letting her family down, being disloyal to her husband, and not being a good mother. She felt useless because she felt she had been a failure.

The turning point came when the behaviour was named, and Mary accepted both her own and her husband's role in this. Naming the behaviour was only possible in the safety of the therapy room, because Mary needed support and witness from an outside source. She was not yet ready to acknowledge her situation outside these confidential boundaries.

Naming the behaviour, becoming conscious of her own role in it and accepting that her husband had been bullying her, took the unnamed, unidentified and unconscious material, which had been causing her such pain, and enabled her to put it into the outside world where she and others could see it, reflect on it and confront it.

CHAPTER 7
RELATIONSHIPS

How can we know the dancer
from the dance?

The child becomes what she experiences. The family is the first social group that the child experiences and it is the basis for all the relationships that she will form in her life. It will influence her ability to participate in groups and to accept authority, and it will have a big bearing on how well she can fit in to society in later life. It also has a significant role to play in the way the child adapts to the demands of fitting in at school. A relationship is like a dance. It connects all those who are a part of it. It is a continually changing matrix of interlinked and interchanging energy and people. The behaviour of each person in it affects all the others and at the same time is affected by the others. It eventually takes on a life of its own. Any change in the behaviour of one element in the relationship will result in a change in the behaviour of the other. Whatever the parents bring to a relationship will directly influence the behaviour of the children, and the ability of the children to relate to other people. The effective child is one who is an active part of the family group, who relates to the adults and other children in the group in an active way, without feeling under threat, or without causing others to feel under threat.

All successful relationships involve a two-way process, with each person asserting and conceding, giving and taking and talking and listening. Successful relationships are based on acceptance of the other person's point of view, acceptance of the other person as a person in their own right and acceptance of difference. This acceptance of other is essential to the workability of any relationship, and it hinges on being able to accept oneself as a person in the first place. The perception of others as a threat to our survival results from not having a strong enough sense of our own identity, worth and place in the world; this will always be a barrier to communication on an equal basis with other people. If the parent or teacher is not secure in their own sense of who they are, then they will have difficulty allowing the child that freedom and will tend to see it as a threat when the child asserts herself or stands up for herself.

All successful relationships need open lines of communication. This means that there has to be a real, live, emotional connection between the people involved in the relationship. This connection has to be verbal, physical and emotional. The child needs to feel that she is being listened to and being heard. Active listening is connecting with the child as she speaks, hearing the words and actively trying to pick up what she means. It tells the child that what she has to say is important and worthwhile and that she herself is therefore important and worthwhile.

All successful relationships need an 'awareness of other', whereby each person has a well developed sense of his own identity as well as a well developed sense of the other person's needs in terms of space and time, both from an emotional and physical point of view. It requires the ability to be able to allow the other person the space that she requires without feeling that she is encroaching on our space. Being secure in our own space comes from knowing that those around us care for us and will support and defend us when necessary. It comes from the knowledge that our boundaries are firm and undamaged and that these boundaries are dependable. But the child needs to know that within the boundaries she has her own space, and that there is room for others within the boundaries without threatening her space. It is about being able to hold the balance of being vulnerable and yet feeling safe at the same time. The effective child acquires the ability to connect, to listen, and to hear, mainly through seeing it in practice and through being a part of it, in action.

Relating to another person involves being able to give up a part of ourselves without feeling that we will be damaged by it. It means trusting that other person who is holding that part of us, and at the same time being able to accept a part of the other person and hold it in trust without feeling the need to own or control it. The effective child can do this, because she is encouraged to have confidence in herself and in the other members of the group.

A successful relationship can balance the ability to concede with an ability to be assertive, without wanting to dominate. It means accepting that the other person's point of view is not inferior, just different. It means knowing that my own point of view is not inferior, just different. It means having the knowledge that even though my point of view is different, it is worthwhile, and I can express it. It also means that I don't feel threatened by other different points of view.

Relationships also depend on the way in which parents and children view themselves and each other. The process of the relationship begins with the parents, and how they see themselves as individuals, how they perceive their children, how they see themselves as group members, and how they view their family in relation to society as a whole. Where parents or teachers are afraid or feel unsure of what they are doing, this uncertainty will be transmitted to the child and will make her unsure of what she is doing and what her parents are doing. Such uncertainty leads to rigid and domineering parenting, where the adult is afraid to allow her ideas to be challenged because she herself does not have confidence in them to begin with. The model of relating which is presented to the child is then one of force and coercion rather than one of cooperation and compromise. Relating is about flexibility not rigidity, it is about acknowledging difference rather than being sure you are right.

Being able to see themselves as separate people, separate from their children, separate from their parents and separate from their partner is also important, because it confers this same freedom on the child as well. Where the relationship between adult and child is too close, we have what is termed 'idealisation'. This means that the child does not see herself as having any identity, importance, or value except in the context of her connection to her parents. This is tantamount to having a non-relationship with another person who is physically separate from the child, but who in effect is psychologically fused with her.

The key element in this is the way in which the family model of relationships operates. It is the system which works successfully which will be adopted by the child when she is required to leave the family group and become involved in other, more competitive groups. The child's ability to form and maintain relationships will depend on how she sees other members of her family relate to each other. It is not what we tell the child to do that counts. It is not what we force them to do that counts. It is the way in which we run our family, the things we normally do, the 'accepted modes of behaviour' in the family that the child will revert to when she needs to in later life.

If it is a 'bad' model of relating, where the norm is rigid hierarchical structures, with no discussion, and where respect is based on position and status, which we present to the child, then it is this model that she will reproduce. If it is a 'good' model, where the norm is negotiation, discussion and respect for the other side, then it is this model which she will reproduce.

Probably the most talked about relationship of all is the bullying relationship. Though not always seen as such, it is a type of relationship and needs to be viewed as such. There is a temptation to believe that bullying only occurs at school. But the fact is that bullying can occur anywhere there are people together. It happens in school, in the workplace, on the sports field and even at home. So what is it and where do we learn it? To a very small degree, we can say that bullying is transmitted through the genes in that there is an certain predisposition in each one of us to bully and to be bullied. It is more that we are all born with an instinct to survive and to protect ourselves. Where this instinct is uncontrolled and allowed free reign, it becomes bullying behaviour. In the situation where the instinct to survive is perhaps not as strong or has not been allowed to develop, the person may be more prone to being bullied. Given the right situation, each one of us is capable of being a bully or of being bullied. This potential is not the same for all people and we can say that some people are more likely to bully and that some are more prone to being bullied than others.

But for the most part, bullying is learned behaviour. It is behaviour that is copied by people who have seen it working successfully. It is a model of behaviour and relating which the child or adult has either experienced directly or observed at second hand, and that she has seen achieving its ends.

The person who bullies another is a person who has a very low sense of her own worth and very strong feelings of inadequacy. This manifests itself in a continuous and powerful need to prove that she is as good as, or better than the other person. It is also based in the fact that the person who bullies feels threatened by the presence of another person near or in her space. This other person may not in reality be a threat, but the bully perceives her as such and is unable to relate to her on equal terms. The only way she feels able to relate is by reducing the other person to a level that she can cope with. Though the bully-bullied relationship is a dysfunctional and destructive one, where there is no intention to give and take, but only to damage and to dominate, it is not a one-sided relationship. The person on the receiving end is also a part of the relationship. As we will see in dealing with a bullying situation, it is the acceptance by the 'bullied' that she has a part to play which is crucial to solving the problem.

This type of relationship is quite closely mirrored in the relationship which the child has with the computer screen, where she has the total control over the conditions of the relationship and can switch on and off when she likes. The computer–child relationship is in other words a totally selfish 'relationship'. It is this type of selfish relationship which is the essence of the bullying relationship, because the bully takes no account of the feelings of the other person.

Part of the mechanics of bullying is that the person doing the bullying takes away the power of the person she is bullying and replaces it with fear, a fear which feeds her own need to prove herself and her spurious need for power and domination. The position of the person who is commonly termed the victim, but who would more accurately be called the 'bullied', is one of passivity, acquiescence and fear. This contributes in no small way to the feelings of 'satisfaction' which the person doing the bullying feeds on. However, the person on the receiving end of bullying behaviour is to some degree the victim of her own passivity and it is in some measure because the bully is allowed to bully that she does so. The shy, unassertive person who may be uncomfortable with dealing with conflict is more liable to be on the receiving of the bullying behaviour. In the bully-bullied relationship, the two factors of power and fear are mixed. Both suffer from fear, but in different ways and for different reasons. One is powerless and is 'content' to remain so. The other, the person who is bullying, is also really powerless but achieves a spurious power to cover up for his feelings of powerlessness, by instilling fear into the other person.

The dynamics of bullying are unconscious in both 'participants'. In other words, the person who is the active participant in the relationship will rarely accept that what she is doing is bullying, while the 'passive' participant in the relationship will often know that there is something wrong, but either be unwilling or unable to name the behaviour. In dealing with the bullying situation, as we will see, it is in naming the behaviour that we begin to change things.

In the world of the bully, both participants take on certain roles and become fixed in each other's view of things as either powerful, strong and dangerous or weak, afraid and passive. Each one develops a perception of both herself and the other person as being powerful, weak, passive, aggressive, afraid, unafraid. They become habituated to these perceptions and at home with them, and will resist moving away from them.

How To Deal With Bullying

There are a number of essentials when dealing with bullying.

Find out what is actually happening. Are the words being used by the child describing the activity accurately? In other words is it really bullying, or is it teasing, name calling? These may be on the continuum of bullying but they are not the same as bullying.

The person bullying has needs which are just as important as the needs of the person being bullied.

The solution to the problem lies within the person herself, both within the bully and within the person being bullied. No-one else can solve the problem for the person who is being bullied, though the intervention of an outside agent will be required.

The basic ingredients of bullying are power and fear. It is these two things that need to be challenged.

Intervention by an outside agent is always necessary, because for the most part both bully and bullied may be happy to remain in the roles which they fill. It will take an outsider to bring the two people to an awareness of what is going on.

The essence of dealing with bullying is taking back one's power without threatening the other person.

Steps For Dealing With Bullying Behaviour

Bring the 'participants' together.

Name the behaviour, of both participants.

Get them to own their behaviour.

Remember both have behaviour to own, both have contributed to the situation, and both have a role to play in changing the behaviour. It is important to accept that the 'bullying' behaviour is as much a form of behaviour as the 'bullied' behaviour and it requires as much intervention.

Make space for the people to own their behaviour without engaging in more bullying behaviour. In other words, if there is a threat of punishment the children/adults involved will find it difficult to own their behaviour.

Bring in an outside agent to demystify the perceptions of fear and power which exist between the two people.

Use role play if necessary to show what is happening and what you feel should happen.

Teach the children the language of negotiation rather than the language of confrontation.

Teach them to stand up for themselves by using:

- Assertive language.
- Assertive gestures.
- Eye contact.
- Firm voice.
- Strong stance.

Relationships and the Effective Child: The Parents' Role

In the busy daily routine of parenting, it is often difficult for parents to find the time to be with their child. There are so many issues and aspects to it that it is a very demanding role. As parents, we are the teachers of relationships, our family grouping is the model which teaches the child how to relate, and the way we communicate with our child influences the way our relationship with them develops and also how effectively the child can form and maintain relationships in later life. Talking with the child is much more inclusive and engaging than talking to the child. The language and vocabulary of relationships is open, soft and accepting rather than closed, hard and demanding.

- 'Can you' is better than 'Do this now'.
- 'It would be a help if you' is better than 'I want'.
- 'I need you to' is better than 'Because I say so'.
- 'I would like you to' is better than 'If you don't I will'.

The language we use and the other ways in which we communicate with our children tell the child a lot about our relationship with them. Just as important is the way in which we listen. Family life has become so busy and so full of things to do that it can be difficult to have the time to listen. Parents may sometimes find it difficult to pay attention to what the child is really saying, and the tendency may be to dismiss or not to take heed of it. Listening involves attending to the child as he speaks, making eye contact, reflecting on what the child is saying, and taking account of the content of what he has said. As often as possible we should attend only to what the child is saying, how she is saying it and what it means, and in doing this put all other things out of our sphere of attention. Where this is not possible, we can ask the child to talk later.

In teaching the child about relationships and in passing on to her the skills of forming and developing relationships, it is essential to show the value of personal space. By being comfortable in our own space and by being at ease when the child or other family members are 'alone', by not always wanting to know what the child is doing, thinking or saying, we are sending the message that it is OK to be on your own. Personal space is not just physically being on one's own. It is often very satisfying to be in a room with your child while at the same time being separate in that both people are 'in their own world'.

In our role as the 'facilitators' of the child's ability to relate, it is the way in which we as adults, parents and people relate to others that will influence the child the most. If we hug our children, laugh with them, cry with them, touch them and are open with our feelings with them then our children will do likewise.

The following may be helpful:

- Allow your child to express his opinions.
- Encourage your child to express his feelings.
- Take note of your child's moods.
- Always leave some room to manoeuvre where there is disagreement.
- Don't ridicule your child or his opinions or feelings.
- Don't hide your feelings.
- Teach the children that being different is good.

It is helpful if parents are aware of their own behaviour. It is possible that you are modelling bullying behaviour to your children. Because so much of it is unconscious, it may be that you are unaware that you are presenting your child with a model which encourages bullying behaviour.

Children can become very adept at bullying their parents, and parents often become so accustomed to this that they accept it, and the children assume it is normal. In preventing this, it is a good idea to take stock once in a while and ask the question: 'What is really going on here right now?'

Relationships and the Effective Child: The Teacher's Role

In the busy, demanding schedule of the modern classroom, the pressure to get 'the work' done is often intense. As teachers we feel obliged to meet the demands of parents, school, inspectors and others. The curriculum in primary schools especially has broadened to include many 'extras', and there is very little time to simply talk. But if we want to 'teach' children to form relationships, we should allow them to practise it in the classroom. To do this they need space and time to talk, to argue and to negotiate on their own, as well as with the teacher as a facilitator. The children are more likely to say what they think to each other than to an adult and this gives us the opportunity to hear what the children are really saying.

Take time to talk with the children by having a time when you are an ordinary member of the group. This can be difficult for teachers, because it involves in some degree the teacher leaving aside his role and status as teacher and advisor in the classroom. Circle time is a useful opportunity to do this, because it affords the teacher the chance to be a part of the circle and yet he will not lose any credibility.

Trust is an essential basis for forming and maintaining a relationship, but it may often be difficult for the teacher to believe what the child is saying. If we believe and trust the child, we show him that he is credible and trustworthy, and we help him to have an open and equal relationship. It often seems more practical to ask other children or adults if we are uncertain about what a child is telling us. This sends negative messages to the child and leads to defensiveness and evasiveness and causes 'relationships' which are based on suspicion and fear. However difficult it is, and however unlikely it may seem, it is vital that our first reaction is to believe the child. If we eventually find out that the child is not telling the truth, then we can deal with that.

Many problems arise in the environment of the close physical, emotional and social contact of the classroom, where children who are perceived to be different in some way may be isolated or excluded by the main body of the group. The difference which is picked on may be physical, and children often hone in on any form of physical difference or disability, such as speech, physical appearance or even something as simple as colour of hair. But it may also be difference related to ability, where a child who is very bright, and gets his work done before others, or a child who is weak and is unable to do his work without help, may be singled out by the group. For this reason, it is essential to create a classroom/school environment where difference is respected and valued. In providing a difference-oriented environment these may be helpful:

- Try to develop a whole school approach to learning difficulty, where the whole staff are involved with remedial, special and resource teaching. Try not to have special needs children or special needs teaching associated with just one teacher or one area of the school.
- Encourage a cooperative rather than a competitive atmosphere in the school. Where possible, allow the children to help each other. The old idea that 'copying is bad' could be modified to allow children to share what they know.
- If children usually have to leave the mainstream for special needs teaching, try to bring the special needs teacher into the class.
- If an opportunity presents itself, allow the good readers, or the better pupils, to avail of the services of the special needs teacher.

Where bullying or other forms of damaging relationships occur, it is important not to put off dealing with the situation. If we defer or avoid facing up to issues of bullying, conflict or any form of unacceptable behaviour, it may result in the children (especially the child on the receiving end) learning that the way to deal with conflict is to avoid it or to run away from it. A very helpful, and indeed time-saving, idea is to oversee or facilitate the children's own dealing with the issue. As far as possible, all the children should be involved in discussions about bullying. It is important to try to treat the person who is 'doing the bullying' with dignity and to avoid ridiculing or isolating the bully. It is much more helpful to the development of healthy relationships if the protagonists are included at all times.

THINGS TO WATCH FOR

- Unreasonable behaviour at home or in the classroom.
- Parents/teachers/children always wanting or getting their own way.
- Parents/teachers/children always giving in, being too agreeable.
- Children who never want to share attention.
- Children who never like to follow rules.
- Children or adults who never break the rules.
- Children who are unwilling to take their turn.

Patrick's Story

Patrick was six years old, in Senior Infants, and the youngest of three children. He was a bright, intuitive child who had no trouble with his work in school. In the playground, however, Patrick could not relate to the other children, would not mix and did not engage in any form of social play. The apparent reason for this was that he spent each playtime in a distressed state, crying and looking for his mother. Patrick's mother told of how he bullied the entire family at home. He controlled where the family sat, which programmes they watched, even what food he ate and when his parents could go out. He had total control of his environment, and if this was challenged or threatened he threw tantrums in order to get his own way. This had begun when Patrick was born, as he was hospitalised due to illness and the latent sympathy for him became the norm. Patrick became habituated to 'specialised' treatment and expected it as of right. In other words, he thought it was normal to behave the way he behaved.

The problem for Patrick was that he had total control at home, because everybody colluded with him, but he couldn't cope when this was denied, as it was in the playground, where he was required to share space, toys, and attention with other boys. So he resorted to the behaviour which was most effective in getting him what he wanted at home, namely, that of the helpless, vulnerable victim, with all the accompanying props of tears, crying and appealing to mammy. While Patrick's behaviour appeared to get him what he wanted at home, it was a barrier to any form of social integration in the real world of the playground.

Two things were important for Patrick's story: (1) involvement of his family; and (2) enabling him to satisfy his needs without resorting to bullying behaviour. My position as therapist enabled both Patrick and his family to have an outside arbiter whom they could both trust and rely on for support.

Play therapy enabled Patrick to develop a sense of being valuable for who he was, without having to put on the persona of the vulnerable, helpless little boy. Whenever this behaviour surfaced, it was possible to challenge it, within the safe confidential boundary of the therapy room. For Patrick, it was essential that he felt that the contents of our sessions were kept within the room, and his parents were happy to accept this. During the course of Patrick's therapy, we had many family meetings where all members were free to have their say and to be heard. This facilitated the changing of the dynamics of the family relationship from the one-sidedness of Patrick's bullying days to the more open and inclusive situation where each one could have their say and also allow the others to have their say.

CHAPTER 8
SELF-ESTEEM AND HOW TO ACHIEVE IT

It's easier to create effective children than to repair faulty adults.

If we can imagine blending all the 'self' words, such as self-concept, self-worth, self-image, the result would be self-esteem. It is the word which best sums up all the various ideas about the self and although it does not mean exactly the same as each one, it contains a little of each. It has, however, become one of the most used word of our time. It is being put forward as the explanation for many of the ills and many of the good things in both children and adults. So what is it and where do we get it from?

Self-esteem is what we think of ourselves, what we think we can do, what we think others think of us. It is about the value we put on ourselves in terms of our ability to influence both our own life and our environment. It is our overall sense of personal effectiveness, what we back ourselves to do, and the emotional value that we attach to our sense of personal effectiveness.

There is a strong emotional element in self-esteem, which is strongly linked with the way in which we acquire self-esteem. The affect or emotion which we associate with particular incidents when they originally happened to us as children, when we were beginning to develop our view of ourselves, is stored in our affective memory just as the incidents themselves are. So the feelings associated with the way we were treated and what was 'done to us', are remembered, and these emotional traces will be reactivated every time a particular incident is recalled or every time a particular incident is repeated. The emotions can be triggered, even though the person is not consciously aware of the original incident or behaviour which caused the feeling. The emotional aspect of self-esteem is what gives it such power and makes it such an important part of the person's overall view of himself.

Our image of ourselves is a function of our parents' image of themselves. The deep emotional bond between parent and child means that what the parents pass on to their children will contain a high degree of emotion. The way in which parents behave towards their children, how they treat them, the messages they send to them, all carry emotional undertones. The emotions and feelings which children experience as a result of their parents' behaviour towards them will remain in the child's psyche as part of the memory and will become part of the child's own perception of himself.

Self-esteem is a 'process', not a product which can be acquired through a quick fix as if we were buying it in a supermarket. It is a continuing process, which begins in the womb. The most important factor in the development of a child's self-esteem is what the parents think of the child. It is the overall view of what the parents think their child is worth, what he can do, the amount of confidence they have in him to achieve — and most of all the way in which he is accepted as a worthwhile individual in his own right. This is presented to the child through the parents' responses and reactions to what he says, does and thinks. It is the reaction of the parent to the child's behaviour and the child's emotional response to this reaction which informs the child what the parent thinks of his behaviour and his capability, and indeed what the parent thinks of him as a person.

The child internalises and assimilates this and it becomes the cornerstone of his own view of himself. It is what the parents reflect back to the child about himself which becomes what the child thinks of himself. The key element in the development and maintenance of healthy self-esteem in children centres around the ideas of belonging and self acceptance. It has its roots in the way in which the parents see themselves, how well they accept themselves and whether they have confidence in themselves to have a say in their own lives.

It is, of course, not only from parents that we get self-esteem. Up to the stage of starting school, it is true that the family, and in particular the parents, are the significant adults and therefore the main mediators of self-esteem for the child. But as soon as the child begins school, another significant adult comes into the child's life and the picture changes. The child's first teacher in particular will have a major bearing on the child in terms of trust in others, belief in his own ability and confidence to achieve. For many children the teacher is another parent, whose word is often as valued by the child as the word of the parents.

So the teacher and the school play a significant role in the development of the child's self-esteem. The school's role is exactly the same as that of the parents. The way in which the school reacts and responds to the child and to his behaviour sends a message to the child about what society thinks of him. This view is internalised by the child and becomes part of his overall emotional makeup. However, today, there is a third influence. The childminder or nursery teacher is for many families also a significant adult, and in many cases spends as much time with the child as the parent. The role of such a person is important, because she can either undermine or reinforce the work of the parents. Choosing a carer who fits in with the family matrix of values, expectations and modes of behaviour is essential in order to foster rather than damage the child's self-esteem.

The extended family, in particular the grandparents, is also an important mediator of self-esteem. For many young working parents, grandparents provide a ready, accessible and affordable means of childminding. For grandparents, this situation often provides them with the opportunity of second-chance childrearing, and they may seek to make up for the mistakes they made the first time around. This very often works out very well for all concerned, with the child receiving the warmth and love of the family, the grandparents feeling that they are carrying out their responsibilities to their family, and the parents happy in the knowledge that their child is in good hands.

In such a situation, it is important that the parents and the childminding grandparents are on the same wavelength as regards the child's treatment. The relationship between grand-parent and parent has many similarities with the relationship between parent and child, and the grandparents may want to 'parent the parents', which may send conflicting signals to the child. The real parents need to assert their position of being the primary significant adults in the child's life, but in a way which includes the grandparents in the process. The grandparents provide the child with an underpinning sense of being a part of a greater system, and by being involved with their grandchildren, the grandparents achieve a sense of belonging and a knowledge that their future is in good hands.

Self-esteem is important because it is linked to achievement in two ways. Firstly, a child with a healthy level of self-esteem is more likely to do well at school and in life generally than the person with low self-esteem. But children who achieve at school and in life generally will increase their self-esteem levels.

Healthy self-esteem goes hand-in-hand with personal effectiveness and the effective child has a strong sense of himself as a person in his own right. Self-esteem is important also because it means that the child does not feel inferior to the other people in his life. He is therefore able to have normal relationships with the people in his life, in class, in the playground and at home. The child with healthy self-esteem feels positive towards himself and others, has confidence in himself to do things and to have a say in his life. It also means that a person looks forward to the future and has confidence in his ability to handle whatever the future holds. In addition, the child with such a healthy self-view feels that with the support of others in his life, he will be able to cope with uncertainty. Self-esteem is one of the building blocks which help to make up the effective child.

Self-esteem and the Effective Child: The Parents' and Teacher's Role

There are ten areas where both parents and teachers can help to develop healthy levels of self-esteem in children and so help them to become effective children.

1. IDENTITY

A sense of identity is an essential part of helping the child to have a strong sense of himself as a separate and individual person. It means that the child is a separate person, with differences, talents and faults, that he knows his own identity and that he likes what he knows about himself. The following ideas will help the child to establish an identity for himself which he sees as separate from those around him, and to maintain a positive self-view of that identity.

If we encourage the child to look after his own needs, he will develop a strong sense of who he is, and a confidence in this identity. The child's opinions are a mark of who he is and if he is allowed and encouraged to express these, he will take it as a sign that who he is is important.

Having time and space to himself, when he needs it, helps the child to develop a strong view of his own identity.

The child's achievements are indicators to him that he is separate and individual. If we praise these honestly, the child knows that we see him as having a separate identity, and that we value him as such.

Individual identity can only be fully achieved in the context of the family, the school and the extended family. It is important to teach the child about his immediate and extended families. By keeping a pictorial record of the child's life, separate from the other members of his family, the child learns that he has an identity that is separate from that of other members of his family.

Part of the child's sense of identity is his individual skills and talents, and if parents and teachers take pride in these, no matter how unusual or individual they may be, it will encourage the child to be himself.

In helping the child to develop a sense of his own identity, it is not only important that parents take pride in his achievements, but that they do not 'steal' the credit from the child. Hand-in-hand with credit for achievement is the need to help him to take responsibility for his own mistakes. Taking his own behaviour, good and bad, on board is an important part of the child's learning who he is.

2. BELONGING

Hand-in-hand with the child's sense of individuality is the need to feel that he belongs to family, school, community and country. Many of the problems for today's children stem from the fact that the feel they don't belong to society, that they are not a part of society, that it has nothing to do with them. Each of us has a deep, unconscious need to belong to a group, to feel that we are a part of the greater scheme of things. It is essential that parents and teachers be conscious of these needs and put in place procedures which will enable the child to feel that he belongs to the family and to the school. The following tips will help to create an environment where the child can feel he belongs.

If the child is included in family issues as much as possible, it creates a strong feeling for him that 'I belong here, in this group'.

The temptation in the heat of the moment to send a child to his room, to put him outside, is understandable, and may provide immediate respite in a difficult situation. Yet this sends messages of exclusion, isolation and rejection to the child. If parents and teachers can become aware of the long-term effects of isolation for misbehaviour, it will make it easier to deal with misbehaviour within the group, rather than outside it.

Regular family meetings also help the child to feel he is part of the group, and that he has a role to play in it. If children are encouraged to share all family and school triumphs and failures, it enables each child within the group to feel a sense of collective belonging. It is important to be aware of not stealing the thunder of the individual and not allowing the individual to opt out of his responsibility.

3. SECURITY

All children need to feel that they have both a strong and safe emotional and physical boundary around them. We can help to set up and maintain strong and secure boundaries if we are conscious of the following ideas.

By being loyal to the child in a balanced, open and honest way, we are showing the child that he has a back-up and a safety net when things go wrong. It provides the child with a feeling of not being alone and of having someone there for him when he needs it.

If we confide in our child we show that we, the most important adults in the child's life, believe in him and have confidence in him, it shows that we trust him and enables him to trust us and others in his life.

Sometimes, when our child has 'let us down' or caused the family to be upset by his behaviour, or if we are angry at the child, it may be difficult for us to believe him. In such cases, we may be tempted to rely on outsiders to find out about our child, and we may feel it is better to ask his teacher or other parents. This can undo the confidence-building measures which we have been practising and will give the child the message that we don't trust him, or that we trust others more than we trust him. It is much better to ask the child himself.

Listening provides the child with evidence that the parent cares about him and is interested in him. It gives the child a feeling of warmth and security, as it makes him feel included within the boundary of the family.

The times of transition during the day, such as going to school and going to bed, are times when the child may be vulnerable. If there is something upsetting him, these are particularly the times when he may feel insecure. Likewise at a time of major transition such as starting school or moving house, he will need to know that there is a secure emotional boundary around him if he needs it. An important part of this is that there are also times of transition and change in our own lives. We need to be able to accept these, share them with our children, and even to allow the child to give you support, at whatever level is appropriate.

If your child gets into trouble, make sure that he knows that though his behaviour is unacceptable, he is still safe and secure. Your child needs to be able to depend on you even when he has done something which is not acceptable. In some ways, it is when he has done wrong that he needs you the most. It is important that he realises the implications of what he has done and that he learns to accept responsibility for his behaviour, but that he knows that within that framework he still has a place within the boundary of the family.

4. SPACE

As well as having a secure boundary, the child also needs to have the space to develop as an individual in his own right. The secure boundary can become a prison unless there is space within it for the child to be himself. Space refers not just to physical space, but also emotional and psychological space which he feels is his, and to which he can go when he needs to be alone.

It is often a surprise when parents find that their children have not been telling them everything, and parents may feel that they should know all about their child's business. It gives the child a feeling of power and of having his own space if he knows that he can keep some information for himself.

When parents need to know what is going on, the important thing is to give the child space and he will tell you what he needs to tell you. If parents crowd a child in an attempt to get information, or to find out what the child has been up to, it has the effect of making the child defensive and evasive. It is much more effective for both child and parent, and for the relationship between them, to allow the child to have the space to talk.

It gives us a boost as people when we see our children become interested in the same things as we are interested in. Where this happens of itself, we can take it that the child is doing it because he wants to, but there is a danger that parents can want their children to follow the same interests and careers as they did. The important thing here is to be aware of what is going on, and to be conscious of making the child aware of other choices.

When a child is playing happily, it is tempting for adults to muscle in on the child's territory. Adults can benefit from being associated with a happy child, they may feel that the child needs them, they may unconsciously resent the child's happiness, or they may unconsciously want some of the child's happiness to rub off on them. Whatever the reason, it is usually the adults who benefit from this invasion of the child's space. A child playing on his own is enjoying his own company, happy with himself, and it is better for him if adults can just let him be.

Another way to help your child have his own space is to allow him to choose his own friends. There will be times when we will be tempted to intervene and insist that the child play with certain named children and not with others. It is true that children are influenced by the children with whom they play, and it is also important that parents are included in their children's life. Where your child is mixing with a child you do not approve of, it is better to express your feelings to your child and allow him to make the choice, rather than to compel the child to do so.

5. WORTH

Self-esteem depends on the child feeling that she herself has value and worth, in her own right as an individual, and as a member of her family. By allowing the child to have opinions and by allowing her to express them, as well as teaching her to respect the opinions of others, she is enabled to develop a sense that she has something to contribute that will be taken seriously, and therefore that she is a person of worth. As the significant adults in the life of the child, we can help her to develop a sense of worth and merit about herself if we try the following.

The parent-child relationship lends itself to parents taking up a 'because I said so' attitude to opinions. It is important for the child's developing sense of worth that the parents can balance their parental status with allowing the child to have her view of things. It helps if parents see their opinions as opinions, and not as diktats.

The same applies to the children's opinions and however difficult it is, the child is heavily influenced by the importance attached to his opinion by those he values. If parents and teachers take the time and allow the space to hear what the child is saying, it will show the child that they value him. If we value their opinions, we value them. In this context, it is helpful and also easier to teach the child the value of listening. If we listen, then the child is encouraged to do so as well.

Praise is an important element in enabling the child to value herself and her achievements, but it is essential that it is honest praise. Praising for the sake of praising, to be liked, or in order to please the child's parents, is giving the child the wrong view of reality. This is likely to lessen motivation, as well as giving her an inflated sense of herself. It is much wiser and more helpful to the child if praise is merited, consistent and not out of proportion to the achievement.

Along with praise, criticism is a part of a child's developing sense of worth. The child will benefit from knowing that there are some aspects of her which are not perfect. It is useful in this context if both teachers and parents can assess performance and evaluate behaviour without being judgmental towards the child.

One of the most satisfying feelings for a child is to know that her parents and teachers are proud of her. Showing pleasure at a child's performance, without trying to steal her thunder, is a skill which all adults dealing with children need to develop. We can be happy for her without stealing her happiness and sense of achievement.

If we are open to the ideas of the child it will signal to her that we, her parents and teachers, have a certain *'meas'* (value, worth) on her and it will help her to develop feelings of value and worth as regards herself and her ideas.

6. FEELINGS

Feelings are the voice of the inner person, the purest form of individual expression and the one part of the person which can be said to be original. If a child is allowed and encouraged to express his feelings, then he will take it that this is an acceptance that he is a person of value.

Many children do not have the words to express their feelings and it is important that we teach them the vocabulary of feelings.

Touch is an important form of communication and it is mainly from parents that the child learns that hugging is not only permissible, but also nice.

The adults in a child's life should be aware of the so-called negative feelings, anger, frustration, sadness etc. and accept them as things to work with, not as things which should be banned.

Crying is a legitimate form of expression, just as laughing, speaking, arguing and as such it should not be discouraged. If children are allowed to cry when they need to, it affords them the opportunity to express themselves. If we are comfortable with the child crying, it will encourage him to express himself.

7. PLAY

One of the most important things in a child's life is playing. It is his way of switching off from work, his way of relaxing and his recreation. Playing is how a child refreshes himself and recharges his batteries. Play provides the child with opportunities to learn and develop the social and personal skills necessary for living. The role of parents and teachers is to provide opportunities for the child to play, and by their attitude to play to show that play is acceptable.

If parents take the time to play with their child and give him lots of time to play by himself and with other children (where possible without the presence of an adult), it provides the child with opportunities to develop the skills needed for problem solving, negotiation and assertiveness.

Competitive situations within the family between siblings or between families are more likely to engender resentment and jealousy. It is more helpful if the environment at school and at home is one of cooperation and participation, rather than competition and exclusion.

Children will take their attitude to play and recreation and leisure from the significant adults in their life. To be an effective child is to work and to play, and to be comfortable at work and at play. If parents take time for recreation and leisure, both with the children and on their own, it will show the child that this is acceptable behaviour.

There is a surfeit of techno toys and toys which leave little to the imagination of the child, in so far as they do so many things merely at the press of a button. Non-mechanical toys give the child a much greater opportunity to use his imagination, to invent and to experiment, and a good supply of toy people, animals, etc. will give endless hours of imaginative play to the child.

8. SCHOOL

As in all other aspects of the child's life, it is what they see happening rather than what they are told to do which influences children. In relation to school, it is the parents' attitude to school, their interest in the child's work and their trust in the school which helps the child. It is not whether parents spend a lot of time doing homework or visiting the school which is important. It is more valuable if they support the child, be there for him and offer help when it is needed. The following tips will be helpful to both parents and children.

Show an interest in your child's work, without being over-helpful, in your child's school, without being too pushy. It is much better for the child and much easier for the parent to play a supporting rather than a leading role in homework. By getting to know your child's teachers, the child will trust them more and value what they do for him.

If parents and teachers can tailor their expectations to the child's capabilities, then there is a much better chance that the child will succeed at school. For this reason, it is necessary to know the capabilities of each child.

If the child is allowed to handle as far as possible his own problems that arise in school, knowing that the teacher and his parents are there as a support if necessary, it will send messages of confidence and trust to the child.

9. AUTHORITY

Many of the problems which young people experience, and which adults experience in dealing with young people, centre around the way in which people perceive and put into practice the concept of authority.

The way in which a child, and later an adult, feels about authority, and how she reacts to legitimate authority is learned in the home and in the school. The child's attitude comes from the model that he is exposed to in the home and in school. If the model is closed, rigid and dictatorial then the child will copy this and see this as the way to react to authority as a child and the way in which to practise authority as an adult. It will also have the effect of suppressing her ability to express her views and feelings and will not allow her to develop a good opinion of herself. There is a difference between authority and authoritarian and the child can only learn that authority is not a threat to her sense of being an individual if the authority which she experiences is not actually a threat. Where the parenting or teaching is authoritarian, where the child has to do things because 'I say so', and where the adults tolerate no challenge to their position in the family/school, the child will feel threatened. She will react by retreating into her own world, where she will not play an active role in her own life and will not feel free to challenge the boundaries of her reality.

Facilitating the child's need to challenge those whom she sees as the aspirations of her childhood is a necessary springboard in the child's attempts to mature. Being allowed to challenge enables the child to engage in the legitimate and necessary flexing of her emotional, social and psychological muscles and helps her to develop the feeling that it is acceptable to push back the boundaries. This is part of the process of enabling and empowering, which is a crucial tool in the life skills toolkit of the adult. In addition, it provides her with a model of authority where it is seen as normal to challenge, while at the same time generating a feeling of safeness.

Authority is also a safe boundary for a child; if it spills over into the authoritarian, it will become a frightening trap from which she cannot escape. The safety aspect of authority is important, because it is such a powerful idea that if misused, it becomes the very opposite to what it is meant to be. Healthy authority is safe for the child, because it provides her with the message that those in authority care for her. Where safety is totally absent from the authority, it comes across as neglect for the child.

If the child has a strong model of leadership and authority, it will provide her with both security and a guide to how to accept authority and how to make decisions.

If your authority comes not from your position as parent or teacher but from the openness and honesty of your decisions, the child will experience the sense of belonging and caring which comes from enlightened leadership. Where authority is based on the position of the adult, the child learns to be authoritarian and inflexible. If parents and teachers can provide a confident model of leadership, the child will copy this and learn the difference between confidence and arrogance.

The father figure is most important here, as it is mostly through the father figure in the family that the child is exposed to an authority figure. This has added importance because of the decrease in numbers of male teachers in primary school. If the father is absent, then the authority figure may come from an outside source and may be a negative masculine role model.

In providing the child with an effective model of authority, it is important that the family rules should be realistic and should involve all the family. This also applies to school and classroom rules, where the potential for authoritarian decision-making is just as great as it is in the home.

One of the most difficult skills for adults to acquire is the skill of allowing the child to question decisions. It is difficult because it takes up a lot of time and because it is a challenge to our status as grown-ups. If parents and teachers can create a facilitating environment where the opinions, questions and the challenges of the child are acceptable, it will teach the child to value the other side of the argument.

10. RESPONSIBILITY

Responsibility is learned and taught, both in the home and in the school. Children learn the need for responsibility and the way to be responsible mainly through the model of accountability and responsibility to which they are exposed in the family and in the school. Children can only become good at those things which they have practised. So if you want your child to be good at taking on responsibility, then you must give him the opportunities to take on responsibility.

If the child is expected to take responsibility for his own things — school bag, lunchbox, bedroom and clothes — he will develop the habit and the skill of responsibility. It is help-ful if there are set tasks for the child to do around the house each day, as this helps him to accept the normality of carry-ing out tasks. It also unconsciously passes on messages of confidence to the child.

The model of responsibility which we present to the child is the one which he will adopt, and it is therefore important that as parents and teachers we are responsible in our own lives. If parents and teachers are willing to accept lower standards of tidiness, orderliness and organisation, it will encourage the child to take responsibility for his own life.

THINGS TO WATCH FOR

- The child who has an inflated sense of his own ability.
- The child who is afraid to attempt a task.
- The child who is always boasting.
- The child who is obsessively neat and tidy.
- The child who can't cope with getting things wrong.
- The child who does not want to take part in group activities.
- The child who always plays on the fringes of the playground.
- The child who cannot take criticism.
- The child who can't allow others to have a say.
- The child who always takes on tasks that are either too hard or too easy.

David's Story

David is a seven-year-old boy who is in First Class and is very bright and intelligent. When he came to school first, he was very quiet, shy, unassertive and unable to stand up for himself. His way of coping with any distress or difficulty was to retreat into his own world, and to become resentful and angry. His anger was a defence against being 'seen as not measuring up', academically, emotionally or behaviourally. His defensive shell of anger and resentment was activated automatically whenever he felt under threat, by being asked a question which he was afraid he did not know, or by finding himself in a situation he could not cope with.

The coping mechanism that David adopted, when he felt under threat, was to 'clam up'. He would tense his muscles and retreat into a silent shell where he felt safe. His fear of failure was so great that it was preventing him from achieving any success. So David's own behaviour was both the cause and effect of his problem, because it was preventing him from receiving the thing which would make him feel good, that is, achievement satisfaction. This was true of David's behaviour both in the classroom and in the playground.

The secret of changing David was the word 'soft'. His defensive shell was hard and impenetrable and the way through it was with softness and understanding. But determination and persistence and patience were required as well. It was crucial that David knew that I was on his side, that he could trust me and that he knew that I had confidence in him, especially when he went into defensive mode, as this was usually the behaviour which got him into trouble. Once he knew that I accepted him whether he was sullen and angry or when he was open and friendly, then he began to accept that I would not change my opinion of him or stop loving him just because he got a sum wrong. Once the process began, the change took on its own momentum. David then became conscious of the rewards that were available, as well as the fact that there was no need for his defensive shell. He began to realise his capabilities and to believe in himself. His self-esteem began to grow.

An interesting aspect of David's case was the excessive swing which took place. We saw in Barry's story how new skills do not sit easily with the person. They are unused to the new skill, have not had any practice in performing and are generally self-conscious and unaccomplished at putting the new skill into practice. In David's case, he was very taken with his new-found power to be assertive, to say what he wanted and to have a say in his world. But at the same time, because he was inexperienced in doing these things, he sometimes became over-assertive and demanding. It was important not to overreact to this and to realise that it was only a temporary flaunting of his new-found power, and that in time it would return to a more balanced assertiveness.

CHAPTER 9
GOING TO SCHOOL

Seeing your child able to cope on his own brings mixed feelings.

Starting school is a normal event in the life of the child and one for which she can be amply equipped, simply by living and growing in a healthy family situation. It is a normal, healthy rite of passage. A useful and visible demarcation for parents and child, it denotes the readiness of both child and parents to move from the very closed, protected and secure environment of the family out to the open, uncertain and challenging world of society.

Starting school is merely a continuation of the process which began at birth and will continue during the life of the child. It is the process of separation which is both natural and necessary. However, at the same time starting school represents the first tangible, obvious step towards independence by the child outside the realm of the family. It is, for the child, the first opportunity to say to her parents: 'I'm all right. I can do this on my own. I don't need you.' As far as the parents are concerned, there are feelings of sadness, regret and rejection mixed with pride in the fact that the child has now reached this second of the many major transitions which will be a part of her life.

There is an implicit threat to the role and status of the parent; very often the parents' unconscious reaction to this is to project negative feelings and emotions onto the school or the teachers, because they are seen to be supplanting the parent, in the world of the child, as the primary significant adult.

102

It may be the first time that the parent will have experienced competition for the affection of the child. Throughout the child's life, there will always be this 'contest' between her striving for independence and the unconscious attempts of the parents to maintain their parental status and control. It is the balancing of the parents need to be good and effective parents with the child's need to separate and become independent which enables the child to become effective in his environment. The effective child is one who is allowed, encouraged and able to be separate and independent, while at the same time having a close relationship with her parents.

By over-emphasising the getting ready for school, we can create fears in the child's mind which do not exist in the reality of his world. In most cases, the difficulties which children have regarding starting school are the projected fears of the parents. Parents' worries are about how she will cope. Will she like her teacher? Will her teacher like her? Will she be able to do well at her school work? Will she be able to survive among a crowd? These may be natural parental concerns, but the child does not know about them until she picks them up unconsciously from her parents. The child's response is, if mum/dad are worried, there must be a reason. So perhaps I should be worried as well.

In many cases, it is the parents' own experiences of starting school which are unconsciously affecting their attitude to the child at this time. Parents who experienced problems, either personal or academic, at school, can often project the same expectation onto their child when he starts school. If this process is not brought out into conscious awareness, the child will eventually assume the problems of his parents. Our own 'bad' experiences at school are part of our overall psychological baggage, but it is likely that they have been kept hidden in our unconscious and we are not aware of them unless we make an effort to think about them.

When the dominant significant adult in the child's life transmits her feelings towards school to the child, it creates a difficulty for both parent and child. If there is an overt reason, such as a physical threat, then it is easy to identify and to remedy. But where there is no real threat, and the parent is expecting the child to experience the same feelings, neither the child nor the parent knows for sure what is causing the child's anxiety. For the parent it is unconscious and for the child it is not really his problem. This is a difficult situation for both parents and the school because what is happening for the parents is genuine and real, though not conscious. It is part of the psychological and emotional inheritance from their own growing up; the fact that it is there and still operational — that is, influencing their behaviour — means that it is important.

The fact that it may be unconscious in the parent makes it all the more difficult to deal with. It may manifest in over-reaction towards any threat to their child, whether real or imagined. It may show in parents being unable to trust the school to care for their child. Or it may manifest in parents spending more time in the school than they need, not being able to allow the child to come into the school on his own, always being worried that their child is safe. To deal with this, it is helpful if parents can separate their own imagined fears and the cause of them from the actual situation and needs of the child. To do this, parents need to learn as much as they can about the school, talk to other parents and admit their own fears.

The recent focus on early childhood has drawn even more attention to the subject of pre-school education and the social and educational needs of children starting school. The following suggestions give an idea of what a child needs when starting school:

- He needs a strong sense of his own identity.
- He should be able to trust others.
- If he can accept himself as a person and accept others, it will be easier for him to benefit from what school has to offer.
- If the child feels secure in his environment at home, this will give him the confidence and trust to feel secure in the school environment.
- It is possible for even a five-year-old to have a realistic concept of self which enables him to accept that he has limits and can make mistakes. For a child starting school, the knowledge that he is not expected to be superman frees him to be himself.

A common perception of pre-school is that it is a means for your child to gain an advantage in the education 'race', and that children who have attended a pre-school/playschool are in some way better prepared for 'big' school. The first thing to be said is that pre-school education is only necessary, to a large extent, because of the gaps which have developed in the pre-school development of the child due to changes in work patterns, society generally and in family systems. Whether it is because both parents work or because of some inadequacies in the family system, the introduction of formal pre-schooling is intended to do what up to recently was being done in the home.

Pre-school can help the child to attain readiness for school, enabling her to effectively make the break away from the protected environment of the home. It facilitates the separation process involving parent and child, a process which often causes difficulty and anxiety. The most important issue here is the timing of starting school, be it pre-school or school proper. Due to work practices, family situations or simply because the parents want to get rid of the child, there is often a rush to get the child into school. Much emphasis is put on age, ability and whether neighbouring children and the child's friends are going to school. In making a decision about whether your child is ready to start school, the following questions will help.

- Is the child emotionally ready to move out of the security of her home?
- Can the child hold her own in a one-to-one situation with another child?
- How well does she relate in a group of her peers?
- How does she react when her mother leaves her?
- How does her mother react when she leaves her?
- Can she play by herself?
- Can she play with others?
- Can she accept the idea of authority?
- How well does she relate to her father?
- How does she cope with another adult?
- Can she look after her basic personal needs?
- Can she cope when things go wrong?

It is not necessary for a child to be able to fulfil all the above criteria in order to start school, but the child who can do these will be ready to take on the challenge of school and benefit from it.

Pre-schools should be guided by the principle that they are engaged in the process of helping to prepare the child to take advantage of what the education system will have to offer. Their programmes should include:

- Confidence building programmes.
- A strong emphasis on language development.
- Lots of talking.
- Freedom to express opinions, ideas and feelings either through art, talk or drama.
- A strong sense of belonging to the group.
- Opportunities for the child to learn about the give and take of operating in a group.
- Helping the child to learn to share attention.
- Enabling the child to cope with uncertainty.
- Activities which facilitate the development of the right side of the brain: art, music.
- Developing an intuitive approach to thinking.

The question that is important for all parents and teachers is: How can I facilitate the child's negotiation of the transition from home to school? It is not about how you as a parent or a teacher can impose your will on somebody else, or how you as an adult can get the child to do what you want her to do. It is about being aware of the personality type of the child, her academic capability and her emotional needs as these relate to the child herself. It is a matter of parents and teachers playing second fiddle to the needs of the child, in order to allow her to make the best of what school has to offer.

Much of what we have said regarding starting school also applies to going to school. Having got over the major transition of starting school, there remains the continuing process of going to school. How much homework should there be? How much parental involvement should there be? Then there are issues such as transferring to secondary school, points and going to college, or indeed not doing so.

School is a place where children learn to learn. It is about the attitudes which children acquire and the importance of the learning process. It is about learning how to learn and how we can acquire information. It is about learning how to adapt, how to relate and how to be a part of a group, as well as learning the value of being able to be by oneself. It is about learning how to accept authority, while at the same time not giving up one's individuality.

Currently, our schools are being run with an emphasis on what we call left-brain thinking. That is, there is more emphasis on those aspects of knowledge and training which are based in the left side of the brain. Current research shows that this kind of approach is only dealing with half of the potential of the person. The left side of the brain is where the logical thinking, sequential skills, reading skills and mathematical skills are based. It is the right brain that is the creative, intuitive, artistic and feeling side. In our schools at present, the bias in favour of left-brain skills and activities is resulting in neglect of the intuitive, creative and emotional intelligence. Not only does the right brain provide balance for the individual, but it also provides balance in the collective or in society as a whole.

The left-brain dominance of the school system has percolated to the family, where the pressure to compete, to perform and to gain points has become the driving force for many parents. The result is that expectations have become almost completely performance based, examination oriented and defined by performance on measurable pencil-and-paper tests. It follows that the inner well-being of the child is being neglected and very little attention is being paid to the emotional, creative, musical and artistic side of the person.

The effective child is one who is equipped to take advantage of what school has to offer. She comes to school ready to avail of the resources of the school, the teachers, the other pupils and the overall human resources. The school should be a facilitating space for the child, a place where the growth of an effective child is facilitated. It should be a potential space, where achievement and achievement satisfaction are possible. It should be a safe space, where the child will feel free to become an effective agent in her own life.

School and the Effective Child: The Parents' Role

Starting school is a time of anxiety and sadness for both child and parent, and if you are upset at your child going to school it is much better not to hide it from her. In the same way, allow the child to express her feelings about separating. Separation anxiety is a part of living which children experience at times of separation from their parents, and it is not something to be avoided or hidden.

When a child starts school, it is important that we let her 'go' to school. It is not enough that we bring her into the school building and present her to the teacher, as in physically letting go. There is also a psychological and emotional letting go, which is just as important. To facilitate the child's move from the secure, protected environment of the home into the more open and unprotected environment of the school, where he will be more vulnerable and exposed to the 'dangers' of society, the parent needs to show her confidence in the child to cope and in the school to accommodate him. We can help the child to make the transition if we become conscious of our own fears about starting school and if we become aware of our unconscious need to hold on to the child.

For many reasons including our own experience of starting school, we may have difficulty trusting the school to be 'good enough' for our child. There may be genuine reasons why we cannot trust the school, so it is essential that we get to know the school and its teachers and that if we have difficulty we address it with the school. Whatever fears we may have, conscious or unconscious, they will be transmitted to the child, unless we bring them to our consciousness and deal with them.

Our child is our guarantee of the future and as such her well-being and welfare are at least as important to us as our own welfare. We want the best there is for our child, and it is often difficult for us to balance our hopes, ambitions and expectations for our child with the reality of the child's capability and the school's effectiveness. We may have difficulty accepting that our child's teacher is not perfect, or that the teacher may not fit our view of what is good for our child. School is a microcosm of the society we live in and is shaped by the society in which it operates. It will therefore reflect the good and bad aspects of the society in which it exists. During his time at school, your child will encounter teachers to whom he relates well, and teachers to whom he does not relate well. This reflects life as it is outside school, and helps the child to learn that it is possible to live with and work with people we disagree with. This is not the same as allowing our children to be taught by 'bad' teachers.

Your child will learn many new things at school, some of which may not be acceptable to you. It is understandable that the parents of a child who has just started school will want to know all about it. But your child may not want to tell you everything that happens. The fact that your child does not wish to tell you everything is a statement by your child that 'I am growing up and I don't need you as much as I used to'.

It is also important to keep your child informed about what is happening. Starting school is an uncertain time for the child, and we will add to the uncertainty if we do not tell him what is happening. It is sometimes tempting to tell the child a convenient story just to avoid a difficult situation. It is better to face the real situation, and if it is difficult for the child to accept the truth, as long as there is someone there to support him he will learn to accept that things will not always be the way he wants them to be.

By trying to recall our own first days at school, and comparing your experience with that of your child, it will help to validate both your own and the child's experience, and to separate the child's experience from yours.

Parents can facilitate their child's entry to school by:

- Bringing her to school, but not into school.
- Getting to know her teacher.
- Talking about her view of school.
- Not crowding her.
- Letting her have her 'secrets' about school. This gives her space.
- Showing an interest in her work but not doing it for her. If it is necessary, do it with her.

A child starting school is an amalgam of his parents' physical, emotional and intellectual makeup. It is necessary that parents try to separate their own abilities and talents from those of the child. This will help to separate your own expectations for yourself from those of your child and enable you to have expectations which reflect your child's capabilities and needs.

School and the Effective Child: The Teacher's Role

When parents entrust their children to the school at five years of age, they are expressing confidence in the system, and it can sometimes be difficult for teachers to honour this confidence. Parental fears and doubts are a part of the process of schooling and education and it is more effective if as teachers we acknowledge this and do not perceive them as a threat to the school or to the teacher.

Schools can alleviate fear and feelings of insecurity among parents if they provide a forum for parents to talk about what is going on and a place for parents to express their feelings. If we resist and try to suppress communication and expression we create anger and frustration and increase the sense of isolation and powerlessness of the parents. By being open and offering parents the chance to have their say, we create feelings of empowerment among parents which are in turn 'given' to the child. By providing opportunities for parents to talk about their fears, it helps the school to know about and to deal with them; it also helps the parents to feel that they are being listened to.

If we can open our schools to parents, by being open about our work, our fears and our needs as professionals, it is likely that schools will benefit from having such a positive energy generated by the goodwill of the parents.

When a child is sent to school by her parents, she brings with her much of the family baggage. Because this is largely unconscious, we fail to separate the child from the family, and without realising it we may ascribe negative or positive family traits to a child simply because he bears the same surname. In trying to ensure that the child is seen as separate from her parents, we can start by ensuring that we do not criticise or blame the child for the parents' behaviour; nor should we put responsibility for the child's behaviour on the parents.

THINGS TO WATCH FOR

- The child who is never allowed to come to school by herself.
- The child who is full of energy on Saturday and Sunday, but not on any other day.
- The child who never says anything about school/home.
- The child who is always in a 'fantasy'.
- The child who doesn't want to go home.
- The child who is always unhappy going to school.

Jack's Story

Jack was twelve, an only child whose parents had separated in acrimonious circumstances, who was coming to the end of primary school. He lived with his mother, but his father had weekly access. His school work had begun to deteriorate and he was losing interest in school, his family and himself. He had become difficult to handle both at home and in school.

Jack's parents' separation had been difficult and much of the ill feeling, mistrust and anger between them had not been dealt with, and still remained underneath the surface. Because they did not live together and rarely saw each other, they were unaware of this. The problem became Jack's, because he became the carrier of the parents' unconscious feelings towards each other. Jack knew that there was something causing him to be angry and upset, but was unaware of what it was.

The key to helping Jack's family was in enabling them to bring to conscious awareness the feelings of hurt, anger and resentment which were active in the unconscious and which each adult was projecting through Jack onto the other. By acknowledging that if they continued as they were they would hurt Jack more than each other, they found the will to withdraw their projections and to include each other and Jack in decisions

---

113

that affected him. An unplanned side-effect was that both parents experienced an improvement in their own lives, which had a further positive effect on their relationship with Jack.

CHAPTER 10
ACHIEVEMENT, AMBITION AND MASTERY

We are good at the things we like and like the things we are good at.

The feelings of mastery, power and satisfaction with achievement are basic needs in children. It is through experiencing these that the child develops a sense of personal effectiveness and develops the ability to fend for himself physically, emotionally, socially and educationally. Personal effectiveness is not so much genetically transmitted as environmentally learned. While it is clear that the capacity for personal effectiveness is in some measure present at birth, the main factor in whether a child becomes an effective agent in his own life is environmental. That is, it is something which is learned from his parents, teachers and other significant adults in his life, as well as from his peers. It is the competitive instinct and the survival instinct in parents which is both a help and a hindrance to the child having ambitions of his own, developing mastery skills and achieving satisfying goals for himself.

One of the most difficult things for parents is to be able to separate their own ambition from the child's. A child gets his ambition from his parents more than from any other source. It is by watching and imitating his parents, and by internalising the values and attitudes which they display, that the child develops his own sense of ambition and need to achieve. Some of this is undoubtedly given to the child genetically, but the greater portion is environmentally handed on.

It is both necessary and important that the parents and teachers have ambitions for the children and it is in this way that the child develops his own ambitions. But where the expectations of the parents are not in tune with either the capabilities or the aptitudes of the child, the child is forced to fulfil the ambition of the parent, rather than realising ambitions based on his own pre-dispositions and capabilities. This happens in particular where the ambition of the parents or teachers is overdeveloped, where they are very successful and find it hard to deal with people who are not as clever as they themselves are. A second factor which militates against the child being allowed to achieve his own ambitions is where the natural competitiveness of the parent, teacher or school become displaced and is transferred unconsciously on to the performance of the child. It is as if the adults view the performance of the child as a measure of their own competence and status in the community.

This is seen in the following ways:

- Where parents of children who have just started school become over-concerned when they discover that their child is not on the same page in her reader as other children in her class.
- Where parents find that their child is not doing the same school work as his friend.
- When parents become upset because the child next door is walking or talking before their own child.
- Where parents feel let down because their child has not got the points which they expected him to get.
- Where parents feel upset because the child is not going to university.
- Where the parents feel disappointed that the child is not measuring up to what they had hoped for, the natural competitiveness which is an essential part of our survival

mechanism becomes blurred and is transferred onto the performance of the child. In this situation, the child becomes the unconscious carrier of the adult's own projected need to prove themselves.

Some of these issues may appear to be trivial and insignificant and we may dismiss or ignore them. But they signify attempts to make the child achieve at a level which may be more appropriate for another child rather than for himself.

In developing the child's sense of personal effectiveness and his feelings of competence and mastery, a crucial aspect is that he be allowed to take credit for his own achievements, while at the same time being helped to take responsibility for his own mistakes. Because of the nature of the parent and teacher roles, it is often difficult for them to stand back and allow the child to bask in the glory of his achievements or to allow them to take the credit. The role of parents and teachers involves by definition a proprietary, a caring, as well as a supervisory role. These are necessary for the child to have confidence in the adults and in the adult system. So while the normal 'mentor' role of both parent and teacher is an essential aid to the child developing mastery skills, it is important that it does not become too forceful and directive. It is also essential that the child be allowed to see his achievements as his own and be allowed to take credit for them.

Hand-in-hand with this is that the child needs to learn that there are limits to his capabilities and that he must take responsibility for his 'failures'. Many parents feel let down by their child's perceived lack of achievement and project this disappointment to the child. The child needs to learn as soon as possible that his performance, be it good or bad, is his and his alone and while it has implications for those around him, he is responsible for it.

Of great importance in encouraging achievement and mastery is a willingness to try. This is the ability of the child to have a go, to make an effort, or to attempt something, without the fear of negative criticism if he fails. If a child or adult is afraid to try, then he has little chance of achievement and of course little chance of achievement satisfaction.

The crucial thing in developing a willingness to try is the attitude of parents and teachers to the child's mistakes. If the response is one of negative criticism and judgment, then the child will be afraid to make a mistake. But if the response is that the mistake is the opportunity and that getting something wrong is just a cue to try again, then the child will not have the fear of failure and will feel free to try and therefore to succeed. Fear of failure is generated by the feeling that our performance is for the satisfaction of others and that we are attempting to please others rather than ourselves. Intrinsic motivation, where the child wants to achieve for reasons within himself, and where he feels that his achievements are not linked to parental approval, is essential in developing the willingness to try in children.

Linked to a willingness to try is the confidence to fail, where the child not only does not have a fear of failure, but actually has the confidence to fail. This is best exemplified where the child has the confidence to undertake tasks in the knowledge that he might fail, but with the confidence that it will be OK even if he does. The confidence to fail shows in the child who does not feel under pressure to perform for the satisfaction of others, and who feels that his achievements are his own and are solely for his own benefit.

A very important part of the process of getting children to achieve and to master their environment is to teach them to set goals and targets. Children need goals to help them achieve. The goals should be of course within the capability of the child, that is they should be attainable. They can be either behavioural or performance goals. An important aspect of this is what happens if the goals are not achieved, or when they are achieved. If too much is made of achieving or not achieving, the child will lose any motive to try to attain the goals. While reward is an important incentive in achieving goals, in determining how well motivated the child is and how hard he tries, it is essential that the reward does not become the sole reason for the child's effort. If this becomes the sole reason the child is doing the activity, then as soon as the reward stops the behaviour stops. Bribing children to get them to perform or to achieve is counter-productive, as the child learns to perform for the reward alone and never experiences the satisfaction of doing things for his own internal reasons. Also, if the 'punishment' for not attaining the goal is too severe the child will be too afraid to fail and will not make the attempt.

Equally as important as having and achieving goals is that the child should as much as possible be allowed to do things by and for himself. There is in all adults a need to feel helpful, a need to be needed and a need to look after our children. Sometimes this need overrides the good of the child and we unconsciously interfere when it would be better to allow the child to do the thing by himself. It is often our adult need to have things right, or finished, that makes us take over. As adults, and particularly as parents and teachers, we may be keen to see things complete and orderly and done properly, which can lead to not allowing the child to finish something in his own way and in his own time. If we want our child to become an effective child, it is important that he is allowed to do things for himself with parents and teachers in a supporting role.

One of the key elements in psychological well-being both in adults and children is to have a belief in the future. It is the absence of this 'confidence in tomorrow' which is the root cause of the ennui and apathy which characterises much of modern behaviour. Much of today's world is about having it now and immediate gratification, and often there is no sense for children that it is good to wait, that we have to earn what we get. This ability to defer gratification and to work towards a long-term goal has been absent from the lives of many people. The result is that children demand rather than request, and are not allowed to develop the skill of working towards a long-term goal, of storing up for tomorrow. This is the skill that is necessary for studying. It is also a basic requirement in the workplace, and its absence is one of the main reasons for the frenetic speed of modern living as seen in the way in which speeding on the road has become commonplace. It was exemplified in the past by such things as saving for Christmas, and post office savings stamps. This belief in the future is essential, for children to have ambitions, the need to know that there is a reward for effort and that when you work at something it doesn't have to pay off immediately.

One of the things which we need to watch for is the development of learned helplessness in children. It comes about if we do to much for them, thus sending the signal that we feel they can't do it, as well as not allowing them to develop the skills of doing. If we don't believe that they can 'do it', then we transmit this lack of confidence to the child and he will begin to accept this as the norm. He will become unable and unwilling to try, and we create a dependency which we call learned helplessness. It is as if we teach the child to be helpless, both by our expectation, by our unwillingness to let him do and by our over-eagerness to help.

Mastery, Achievement and the Effective Child: The Parents' Role

There is much discussion about the idea of image and substance and the ways in which real issues are masked or hidden by the way they are presented. Part of our existence is about the way we dress, the way we present ourselves and generally about our appearance. In helping the child to become an effective child, we should try to put more emphasis on what he does and who he is, than we put on his appearance.

Young children can find difficulty in completing a task without spilling something or making a mess in some way. If we can alter our attitude to untidiness and how things look, we will be able to show the child that finishing things is important in itself, and that it is more important that it is finished than that it looks well. Appearance can come after competence.

Often when we find a child busily playing or working, we are tempted to get involved with him, to help or indeed to get the thing finished quickly. It may be our own unconscious need for acceptance and power which motivates us to interfere, but we ascribe more acceptable motives, such as helping, to our behaviour. It is much more helpful to the child and better for developing his personal effectiveness if we allow him to decide if he needs help and only to offer it when he asks.

In developing the effective child, it is much more influential if parents show the child *how* to do something rather than doing it for him. If we show him and then let him do it, we are not only helping him to do it, but are expressing confidence in the child, and developing his own belief in his ability.

We should be conscious of the link between reward and achievement. Firstly there is inevitably a link between reward and achievement in a society where greed and commercialism have led to the expectation of immediate material rewards. Reward is a legitimate motive to encourage the child to achieve, but where the two ideas become too closely linked — and indeed where all achievement is rewarded — the child may think that all achievement has to be rewarded and will try to achieve for the reward only.

One of the things which gives the greatest satisfaction is when we achieve a goal which we have set some time before. The immediacy of gratification, the idea that the child has to be rewarded now, prevents the setting of long-term goals. If parents help in goal-setting, by encouraging long-term goals and by encouraging the perseverance to stick with it to the end, the child will be able to set and achieve goals himself. The most effective help we can give to the child is to set goals in terms of behaviour and achievement which are realistic, based on the child's needs, and which are achievable by the child himself.

If we have one or two long-term goals that allow the child to 'save up', to accumulate or to defer satisfaction, we will teach the child the benefit of working for something; we will teach him that rewards do not have to be immediate and will also enable him to develop a confidence in the future.

Mastery, Achievement and the Effective Child: The Teacher's Role

If we set goals and targets for the class, both collectively and individually, we will show the children the value of working towards a future goal and teach them the value of group goals and of teamwork. We can more easily monitor the suitability of the goals and ensure that the child maintains his commitment to achieving the goal.

When we want to show the child how to achieve and to help him gain the benefits of achievement, it is important to allow the child to take credit for his achievements. He needs to be made aware of what his achievements are, that he is responsible for those achievements, and that the credit for them is his.

In conjunction with this, the teacher should help the child to be aware of his mistakes, and to take the 'credit' for his mistakes. To do this the teacher needs to create a facilitating environment in the classroom where the children will feel that it is OK to make mistakes and to admit to them.

It is often difficult for a teacher not to interfere in a child's work when we can see that he is having difficulty. If the teacher can take a more objective stance, it will allow the child the time and space to finish what he starts. In developing effectiveness in children, one of the most important things is for the child to know both his capabilities and his limitations. He needs to know that he has the ability and the perseverance to finish what he starts. Many children develop the habit of checking each stage to be sure it is 'right' before going on to the next stage. This behaviour takes away the opportunity for the child to see things through to the end and promotes dependency on others. We can teach the child to finish what he starts, by giving time and space to do so.

THINGS TO WATCH FOR

- A child who is so concerned with the appearance of his work that he never gets anything finished.
- The child who asks for help before he begins.
- The child who never finishes work.
- The child who is unable to take credit/praise for his achievements.

- A child who is always looking for a reward for completing a task.
- A child who becomes overly upset when things go wrong.
- The child who tries to hide his mistakes.

Justin's Story

Justin was eighteen, clever, independent and confident. He was a very strong personality with a passion for motorbikes. He was a very talented moto-cross rider and had won many competitions. His parents were concerned about him, as they thought that he was at risk of becoming involved in drug-taking. There was no hard evidence of this, but Justin had moved out of home because of the repeated arguments and fights with his father over his lifestyle. The essence of the problem was that the mother wanted to know where Justin was, what he was doing and with whom, at all times. The mother took Justin's unwillingness to tell her as evidence that there was something to hide, while Justin took his mother and father's unwillingness to believe him as a lack of trust and confidence.

At a family meeting Justin was immediately isolated, unconsciously, by the parents and the father's hostility to Justin and his achievements was very evident. The mother's lack of trust manifested as helplessness, and lack of confidence in Justin to cope on his own. But it was clear that Justin would prefer to be at home with his parents, which is what they also wanted.

Although Justin was a strong character, who knew what he wanted and was extremely brave when it came to riding his motorbike, he was afraid of both his parents, though in different ways. By playing the 'vulnerable/helpless' card, Justin's mother had made him guilty and afraid of hurting or upsetting her, with the result that he was afraid of his mother's fear. His father was so threatened by Justin's independence, and the

---

prospect of losing his position of primacy in the family, that he had frightened Justin away. The important issue here was Justin's fear, because it was allowing his parents to believe that their excessive control was legitimate, and therefore that they did not have to change.

Most of the work was with Justin and it centred on two things. It was necessary to get him to accept that he did not have the right to control his parents, but that if he changed his attitude towards them they would change towards him. We concentrated on getting Justin to see and accept his parents as they were, and to accept that they had the right to be that way. At the same time, we got him to 'psychologically beat up' his father, without in any way denigrating or judging him. When Justin realised that it was OK to disagree with his father and that he did not always need his mother's permission, he became less afraid and more open with his parents. They in turn began to see him differently and were more willing to trust his judgment.

CHAPTER 11
PLAY

Play is the creative space for the child.

Play is important for a number of reasons. Firstly, with the proliferation of mechanical toys there is less place for the inventive play where children make up games and entertain themselves. Secondly, with the increased perception of society as being a dangerous place, there is less free and unsupervised play on the street and in the parks. This leads to more supervised play, whether in the school playground, at home or on the street. Thirdly, play is more and more adopting the rules and ethics of the workplace and is losing the free expression which is essential for it to do what it should do. But most importantly of all, play provides the child with the opportunity to be himself and to experience childhood.

Play should provide a necessary balance to work. With the growing emphasis on work, it has become more important for the child to have her playtime away from adults. This gives the child the chance to learn to deal with her own life situations and to learn to solve her own problems. It provides the child with opportunities to test her own capabilities against her peers and helps to develop a realistic sense of her own ability. Play provides the child with the opportunity to develop the right side of the brain, abilities which may not be catered for in school or at home. It is the child's chance to legitimately escape from the realities of school, home and work.

The Need For Play

The need for play in the human being is really a need for fun. Children and adults need to have a fun element in their lives, to provide a balance to work, and play provides this. But for children it has a more practical function. Play allows the child to imitate the behaviour of the adults in her life and it is through this modelling that the basics of gender are learned. Play also allows the child to work through any anxieties which she has. In the fantasy of play, she can project negative feelings from the threatening object onto the plaything, which helps her to disarm the fearful object. Play also enables the child to gain insights into both herself and those around her, and helps her along the way to knowing her capabilities and her limits. It is a very important aspect in teaching the child the give and take of relationships. She learns that there are limits to what she can get away with, and that if she wants to be a part of the group there are certain concessions that she will have to make.

In group play the child learns the value of personal effectiveness in gaining access to the group, remaining a part of the group and dealing with exclusion. Playing the role of the 'goodie' and the 'baddie' enables the child to experience the feelings associated with having power and being denied power, in situations that do not have serious consequences. The nature of play allows the child to manipulate her environment and to feel that she has a say in her life, while at the same time it does not impose the responsibilities of serious, real life situations on her. Trust is important in the ability to develop and practise the skills of interrelationship, and play provides an opportunity for children to practise trusting others, while at the same time learning that we cannot always trust people. It affords the child the opportunity to practise the skills of negotiation, problem solving and just plain getting along with others.

Types of Play

Play is when the child is completely absorbed in an activity, when she is engaged in it because she enjoys it, when she is having fun. It is intrinsically motivated activity, where the child is doing it because she enjoys it and not because it pleases others. It can be a group activity or it can be a solitary activity. There are many types.

For the most part, the computer has become the modern playmate. Many children have access to a computer or have some derivative of a computer, such as a computer game, in their homes. Playing on a computer is not the same as playing with another person, and though it is certainly classed as playing, there are many differences between playing with a computer and playing with another child or a group of children. The fact that it is usually solitary play is not in itself a drawback. The negative side of 'mechanical play' is the fact that it lacks any form of give and take: the child is in total control of his 'playmate' and it will do exactly as he tells it. This total control by the child may have serious repercussions when he tries to transfer this form of relationship to the outside world of society. In fact, the computer-child relationship does not prepare the child for the reality of the outside world, where she has to concede and give ground. The computer gives instant gratification and there is endless variation if the child requires it.

However, becoming computer literate is part of the overall package of personal effectiveness and as such is a necessary skill in the child's toolkit of life skills.

Social play — playing in a group — is the play which is most common and most beneficial to a child. It is in playing with other children that the child gets closest to what life is going to be like. It is here that she learns how to compromise, how to deal with conflict and how to stand her ground. The less adult supervision the better, because where there is supervision, the child is relieved of the responsibility of dealing with whatever problems arise. In social play, the child learns the skills necessary to gain access to a group, the skills necessary to retain his status in a group and the skills necessary to regain access in the group when he has been put out. These are all skills which are necessary for developing satisfactory relationships, especially in family situations and in the workplace. So it is necessary as far as possible to leave the children to play by themselves and not to interfere. The more they deal with things in their own way, the more they will be able to deal with life situations later on. By allowing children the opportunity to play on their own, we create the need for them to argue, negotiate and to compromise and so allow them to learn and practise these skills.

Fantasy is a characteristic of most children's play, but especially of solitary play. It is important that children are allowed and have opportunities to play by themselves. Parents should not put pressure on children to always be with their friends, as this creates the impression that it is somehow wrong to want to be on your own and it denies the child the opportunity to learn to be happy with her own company. The ability to be at ease with her own company and to be able to amuse herself is a combination of being happy with one's own self-view and being encouraged to spend time in the company of one's own self.

Play fighting is a feature of the modern playground, and is regarded with scepticism and anxiety by both parents and teachers. Perhaps it has acquired a more serious tone, but it is not a new development in children's play. It is a modified form of playing, which incorporates the serious element of the child asserting herself and satisfying her power needs. Play fighting is the child's way of accommodating to the need to include the fun element of play and the serious element of fighting in the one activity. It is a legitimate and healthy form of play, invented by the child to allow her to test her skills of mastery and efficacy in her world. It provides the child with a testing ground where she can test her capability and her image of herself against the real world, in a situation where the consequences are not final. In other words, it is a non-serious way of testing a very serious thesis. It is practice for living.

Another form of play is sport, which forms a significant part of the Irish way of life. Few children will go through life without having some involvement in sport. Sport for children should be just that: fun, enjoyment and play. There is a tendency to make children's sport serious and competitive, with an emphasis on winning competitions, on structure and on appearances. This has led to greater emphasis on coaching and standardisation. The result is that the play element has been taken out of children's sport. The reason for taking part has been changed from the child's enjoyment to the satisfaction of adult ideals. In short, we have turned children's sport into work.

Sport for children should be about participation, fun and mastery of skills, and allowing the child to develop her kinaesthetic abilities and spatial intelligence. It should be an opportunity for her to show off how good she is, to challenge her own view of herself and to learn how to stretch herself a little further each time. There should be no serious competition in children's sport until at least the time when she is finished school. The argument that 'it is a competitive world out there' and children need to learn how to cope with it, is spurious. The effective child will learn all she needs to survive if she is allowed. Competition puts a premium on results, and makes adult approval conditional on winning. It is therefore a negative force in the process of developing children who are effective and active in their own life situations.

Play and the Effective Child: The Parents' Role

It is from parents that a child will get his attitude to play and in some measure his ability to play. Children have an innate ability to play and if left to themselves they will do so happily. More importantly, the ability to play is a good indicator of the child's well-being. It is important that parents play with their children, in order to show the child that it is acceptable behaviour, and because playing with your child helps to develop healthy and open relationships.

If parents encourage and give the chance for free play, it helps to develop creativity and inventiveness. It is important that the child learns to play by himself and that it is not always necessary to be in a group. Being at ease by himself and not feeling that he must always be in the company of his friends is an important aspect of the child's growth. To help the child achieve this, we can provide a space for him to spend time in his own world, encourage him to play by himself and have a quiet time each day when everybody in the house spends some time in their favourite place, or just sitting together without talk or television noise. As the child grows, he will acquire the ability to be happy with his own company and as an adult will be able to be by himself without being lonely. This ability will also enhance the child's sense of his own worth as a person.

Many of the toys that are available in toy shops and which children buy and have bought for them tend to be hard —

plastic or metal — and even toys such as computer games tend to be hard rather than soft. So it is helpful in providing balance in the child's play that soft playthings such as sand, water, plasticine, modelling clay, etc. are provided. In addition, we should try to provide toys which are non-mechanical. Much of the toy market comprises toys which are mechanical, technological and electrical. While these reflect society and provide the child with opportunities to play and to share, it is necessary to provide balance by having toy animals, people and also live pets for the child to play with. The soft toy is a more feeling toy, while the hard toy is a more logical toy.

If parents show children how to relax, to play and to have leisure, then the child will do likewise. If we take time off to relax and if your child sees that you enjoy 'play', then she is more likely to believe in it herself. The child develops his attitudes to play and work from watching us, and if we believe that play is a waste of time or idleness, then the child will develop this attitude towards it.

There are demands and pressures on parents and teachers to supervise children at play. The basis for this is that there are perceived dangers to children if there is no adult present. It is easier for the child to become effective in his own environment, develop skills of negotiation and bargaining as well as the ability to stand up for himself, if he is allowed and encouraged to play without adult supervision as much as possible.

Hothousing — the practice of forcing the child to concentrate on one sport and to spend inordinate amounts of time being coached in this sport in the expectation that she will be professionally successful at it — is mostly associated with other countries. However, the temptation for parents to limit the child's sporting activities to one sport at which she is proficient is noticeable. As in all things in the child's life, balance is required, and it is much more beneficial to the child that she be allowed to play as many sports as possible. It lessens the competitive aspect for the young child and gives a broader view of playing. In allowing the child to play as many types of sport as possible, we are providing a better chance to find an area of recreation which suits her.

Alongside this is the fact that some children do not wish to play organised sport. This is often because they find it too serious, or because they feel they are being shown up in public, especially if they are not adept at physical activity. It is not necessary for every child to take part in organised sport, and where a child objects to so doing, it is important to hear what she is saying. It is, however, also important to ensure that the child has opportunities to play if she wants to. If a parent has been very successful at a particular sport, he may unconsciously expect that the child will follow in his footsteps. It may be that being good at sport will help the child to become effective, but if the child has no aptitude or desire to play, she may resent being pushed into something where she cannot get any achievement satisfaction. Don't force her to play; give her the opportunity.

Highly competitive sport and sport which is excessively structured takes away the pleasure which children need from play. The idea that it is a competitive world out there, and that it is necessary to teach a child to be competitive does not stand up. It is far more valuable to the child if his play experience and his involvement in sport is enjoyable and recreational and based on intrinsic motivation. This will enhance the child's self-esteem and enable him to deal with whatever competitive situations he encounters in later life. Parents will have the greatest influence in the sporting involvement of the child and should try to avoid putting him into highly competitive situations.

Play and the Effective Child: The Teacher's Role

Sport and PE in school offer the teacher the opportunity to provide for the needs of many of the children who may not experience success in the academic life of the classroom. At the same time, it is an area where children can feel isolated and left out. The school can make the sport and PE inclusive and relevant to all the children by:

- Avoiding 'eliminator' type games.
- Making participation more important than winning.
- Rewarding children for participation as well as for achievement.
- Broadening the range of games played to include as many children as possible.
- Including games where strength and physique are not important in order to do well.
- Allowing the children to invent games.

The school's attitude to play is similar to the parents' attitude, because the children take on the attitudes of the adults who are important at the time. Schools can help to develop a positive attitude to play and also help the children to benefit from play by:

- Providing a space for play.
- Giving time to play in addition to the normal 'breaks'.
- Including play and playtime in the school plan.
- Having a positive attitude towards play.

THINGS TO WATCH FOR

- The child who never seems to want to play.
- The child who cannot use symbols or imagination.
- The child who only becomes interested when the computer is in use.
- The child who always wants to win.
- The child who becomes overly aggressive when playing games.
- The child who is over-dependent on rules.
- The child who becomes upset at losing.

Natalie's Story

Natalie is eight, in Second Class, and is the oldest of three children. Attendance at school is very poor, and her mother is the most significant person in her life. She lives at home with both her parents, but her father is rarely seen.

Natalie is unable to sit still in class, finds it extremely difficult to conform to classroom routines and constantly interrupts the work of the class. She is often violent towards her peers, both in the classroom and in the playground. Her changes of mood are sudden, apparently unprovoked and frequent. She appears unable to empathise or to have compassion for those she hurts. She is extremely sensitive to criticism, and although very bright intellectually, rarely experiences any achievement satisfaction, because she rarely completes her work.

Natalie's mother does not relate to her neighbours, she is suspicious of professionals and is unable to separate her own issues from those of Natalie. She feels that any criticism of Natalie is directly aimed at her. The result is that she will always try to fight Natalie's battles, and is resentful of any suggestions about changing the situation. Natalie's mother maintains that there are no issues to be addressed with regard to Natalie's behaviour. She was unwilling to become involved in any process of changing Natalie's world, or her way of dealing with this.

CHAPTER 12
REALISTIC CONCEPT OF SELF

Accepting our limitations gives us the
freedom to achieve our potential.

In developing personal effectiveness in a child, it is necessary that the child has a realistic concept of who he is, what he is capable of and what it is not possible for him to achieve, as well as having some idea of his potential.

'A realistic concept of self' means that the child knows that he 'can do', is willing to try, feels that he has ability, has confidence in this ability and also has the confidence to fail. It also means that he does not have an inflated sense of his ability and is happy with his limitations. All of this comes from the way in which his parents and teachers react to his attempts at achievement, his achievements and his 'failures'.

One of the dangers in this area is the way in which parents may unconsciously want their children to do the things which they themselves failed to do. It is an unconscious attempt to affirm their own sense of competence and mastery and is part of the legitimate transmission of ambition to children. But conscious awareness of the process is necessary if we are to avoid imposing unsuitable and unattainable goals on our children. Unrealistic goals or expectations are expecting the child to do something which is not within his capability and which is not based on the child's needs. The process usually begins with a parent or a teacher whose expectations for the child are based on needs outside the child. Because the parent or teacher is a significant person in the child's life, these expectations are then internalised by the child and become part of his own overall psychological makeup.

When we set unrealistic and unattainable goals for people they are unaware that the goals are unrealistic and believe they should be capable of achieving them. There is often the additional sense of wanting to gain the approval of the significant adult. When they fail, the blame is often taken on by the child, which means that he thinks he is not good enough. It results in lowered self-esteem and a general damaging of the child's sense of his own worth.

Unrealistic parental goals also result in the child setting unrealistic goals for himself, because this saves him from the embarrassment of failing. He sets unrealistic goals for himself in two ways. (1) He will either attempt tasks which are much too difficult for him, in the knowledge that if he fails it will be more acceptable because the task was so difficult in the first place. But by setting very high standards of either behaviour or achievement, the child lessens his chance of success and so reduces the feelings of satisfaction he would get if he succeeded. (2) He will tend to choose very easy tasks, at which he is guaranteed to succeed. But there is no challenge or no sense of satisfaction, and very little approval from those around him, for succeeding at a task which is so easy.

A child who always sets himself unrealistic goals will become more used to 'failure' than success and will become habituated to not achieving. So he will think it normal for others to do better than him and for others to do things for him. This is the opposite of the effective child, who has a good picture of his ability and what he can and can't do. More importantly, he accepts this about himself.

Realistic goals are those which are within the capability of the child and at the same time involve some element of challenge. A task which is too easy presents no challenge and therefore no satisfaction if completed. A task which is too difficult will only result in frustration and failure for the child. Realistic expectations are based more on the ability and makeup of the child than on the demands of his environment. They involve tasks and goals in which there is an element of risk and where there is willingness to let the child use his intuition and guessing skills. Expectations should encourage the child to use as much of his personal effectiveness toolkit as possible, while at the same time being just sufficiently beyond his reach to make him stretch to attain it. He should be aware that he can have help if he needs it, that there will be approval whether he succeeds or 'fails'. The approval is not dependent on success.

As well as an 'I can do' mentality, parents and teachers should be promoting an 'I can't do' attitude. This may seem out of place and negative, but the child needs to know that there are things which he can't do, that it is OK not to be able to do some things, and that it is OK to look for help. This needs to be linked to achievement and ambition so that the child learns that he is capable, as well as knowing that there are limits to his ability. It is important that he feels that his parents and teachers know that he has limits and that they accept him with his limits.

He needs to learn that it is not a reflection on him as a person if there are some things which he cannot do. This will be transmitted to him by his parents' reactions to his attempts at achievement, and especially when those attempts are not successful. The ability to accept that he has limitations, and that these are not negative traits, comes in the first place from the child's view of his parents' reactions to his attempts at doing. So it is essential that parents accept the child as he is and not as they would like him to be. This does not rule out having ambitions and expectations for your child. It just means being able to balance expectation and capability. An important aspect of this process is the ability of parents and teachers to accept their own limitations, and to separate their own abilities and limitations from those of the child.

Learning that he has his own area of competence where he can excel, and that this is not necessarily the same for him as it is for others, is important in the process of acquiring a realistic concept of himself. For this reason, it is important that we are aware of the child's personality type and his aptitudes so that we can give him opportunities in the areas that he is good at. It also teaches the child that he can achieve without having to measure his achievements against the achievements of others. Achievement is not defined in terms of being as good as, or better than, peers or classmates. It is measured in terms of 'how well I am doing in relation to what I am capable of doing'.

The ability to ask for help, which is an admission that one has limitations and imperfections, is something which children often find difficult. This is most often associated with boys, who are conditioned by society always to appear capable and self-reliant. Both are desirable traits in themselves, but it is where they are over-valued that the child is unable to admit that he needs help. There are a number of reasons for this. Our competitive culture sees it as a sign of weakness if a person has to look for help, and the child therefore sees it as not the correct thing to do. It is, of course, important that children learn to be self-sufficient and self-reliant so that they will not be over-dependent on their significant adults. But children who are over-independent and over self-reliant develop an inflated and inaccurate self-concept which makes them feel that asking for help is a sign of weakness and inferiority.

Providing a model of effectiveness is an important role which parents and teachers have to carry out. This is not the same as creating the impression that we are omnipotent, or that we always have answers. It is as much about showing children how to ask for help, how to accept and how to give help, as it is about being competent, capable and having answers when our children need them. It is also about being able to help when help is needed. The child imitates the role model in the home, whether it is an effective or an ineffective model. A lot of what we transmit to our children is done unconsciously, and it is often when we are not aware of the messages we are sending that they are picking up what we do.

As parents and teachers, we are to an extent heroes to the children we have in our care, and as such are models of best practice to our children. As models of personal effectiveness, we show the child how best to cope with reality, how to deal with problems, not how to avoid them, how to be an individual in a group and how to deal with conflict. The model for the child to base his own behaviour on should be one showing how to get things done, how to complete a task and how to share space, attention and objects. It is not by saying or telling that we achieve this, but by being it. It is how we cope with adversity, how we deal with problems and how we run our family system, how we deal with opposition and conflict and generally how we communicate, that the child imitates. This will be the model for the child to follow because when the need arises, it will be this model that he will turn to. It will be the system which he is most comfortable with, because the system he has been reared with will have become built-in to his psychological makeup. If it is a bullying, domineering, closed system, then this is the way in which the child will try to run his life. And if it is an open, cooperative and 'other' oriented system, then this is what he will try to implement in his dealings with the outside world. The family is the first and most influential model of group dynamics that the child encounters, and the way he approaches work, play and relationships in later life will be modelled on what he finds here. The effective child develops a realistic concept of himself by seeing it in action and by being a part of a system where it is active.

The Effective Child and Realistic Concept of Self: The Parents' Role

To help the child achieve personal effectiveness, he needs to have an accurate picture of himself, physically, emotionally and socially; it is very much through his parents that he acquires this picture. If his parents accept the child for who he is, and not so much what he can do, cannot do, may be able to do, or not do, it will enable the child to form an accurate picture of himself. This means seeing the child with all his faults and limitations, as well as his talents and abilities. It means being able to accept the child as he is at this moment, not as we want him to be, but as he is. It means being aware of all his negative aspects, and accepting the child with these. We may hope to change the way the child behaves, but the first step towards change is acceptance of the status quo. His parents can help the child to acquire a realistic idea of himself as a person, by being aware of his abilities, his talents and his achievements and accepting the person with these positive aspects.

If parents can tailor their expectations to fit the child's level of capability, his personality type and his emotional needs, this will help the child to realise that he does not have to achieve what his parents achieved. It will also help him to realise that he doesn't have to attempt to do the impossible.

It is important that parents are aware of their own ambitions and expectations for themselves, in order to separate these from their expectations for the child. It also means that the parents will not submerge their own ambition in the child's performance, and it will allow the parents to pursue their own ambitions. Try to be aware of what your ambitions are for your child and separate your own needs from those of your child.

Being honest with the child when appraising his work helps the child to form an accurate view of what his capabilities are. It is much more beneficial to the child if parents do not praise where it is not merited and do not criticise for the sake of it, in order to reinforce your authority as a parent. A child will pay a lot of attention to the opinions of his parents, though it may often appear otherwise, and if we feed misinformation back to him about his performance, it is likely that he will have an inflated sense of his ability.

One of the more valuable skills that make up the repertoire of the effective child is the ability to finish what he starts. This is very much a learned skill and it is learned for the most part by imitation. If the important adults in the child's life are people who usually see things through to the end, the children will accept this as the norm and assimilate this way of being into his own way of operating. But it is also possible for parents to encourage the child to finish what he starts. If this is something which he finds difficult, and depending on his personality type he may, we can help by shortening the duration of the task and increasing the number of shorter tasks, or by offering an incentive for finishing the task rather than for the quality of the work.

It is valuable to have attainable, realistic short- and long-term goals for your child. If the child is included in the process of setting the goals, he will find it easier to want to achieve them. We can also teach and show the child the value of deferred gratification by encouraging him to save for holidays, birthdays, and Christmas.

To help the child form a realistic view of himself, it is effective if parents challenge and question any inflated or unrealistic self-view which the child may develop. This needs to be done in a non-threatening, non-judgmental and inclusive way. Although the child's self-concept is linked to that of his parents — particularly as regards the formation of his self-concept — it is essential that we do not compare or judge the child's self-concept with our own as parents.

The willingness and ability to accept help from others is a basic requirement in helping the child to develop a realistic concept of himself. If parents accept help in their own lives, without attaching the label of weakness to it, then your child will learn that he can also do it.

The Effective Child and Realistic Concept of Self: The Teacher's Role

The teacher's role in enabling the child to have a realistic concept of himself is almost as crucial as the parents. Setting goals for the child gives her the opportunity to test herself and to measure her ability to achieve against what she thinks she can do. This process shows the child whether or not she is as good as she thinks she is, without any public evaluation. It is valuable in this context to have a list of goals to achieve during the year, and more short-term goals to be achieved before the end of the year. If we draw up a daily plan each morning, the children accept both the collective and individual goals which are set.

Children like the idea of being involved in the planning stage and if teachers can allow the children to set goals for themselves, it not only gives the feeling of inclusion, but it also makes the child more eager to achieve the goal. More importantly, it gives the child practice in the skill of goal setting, something which he will need if he is to become good at it.

One of the pitfalls for teachers in this respect is that children who have low self-esteem or an unrealistic/inflated sense of their own ability will tend to set goals which are very difficult to attain. It is important that the teacher keeps a watching brief to ensure that the goals are within the capability of the children. Teachers can facilitate this process by selecting goals based on the needs and ability levels of the individual child.

If the teacher cultivates an 'I can do it' mentality in the classroom, it will help the child to develop a positive approach to problem solving and not to give up at the first sign of difficulty. To do this, the teacher needs to be non-judgmental when children fail to achieve goals. He needs to be able to provide the children with a model of effectiveness, while showing the ability not to interfere in the child's attempts at self-reliance.

Hand-in-hand with this should be an 'I can't do it' mentality. This means teaching the children the benefit of being able to say 'I can't do it' or 'I need help'. The idea of encouraging the child to admit his limitations may seem to teachers a negative and unproductive strategy, but it provides the basis for realism in the child's view of his ability. It acts as a safeguard against the growth of the superman or superwoman ideal later in life. It helps both the teacher and the child to form a realistic view of the child relative to what he is capable of. The child will copy this, internalise it and assimilate it into his own psychological self-view.

THINGS TO WATCH FOR

- The child who never asks for help.
- The child who always approaches a task with an 'I can't do it' attitude.

- The child who finds it difficult to defer gratification or to have long-term goals.
- The child who has an inflated view of his own ability.
- The child who will not allow others to get credit.

Anne's Story

Anne is eleven and in Fifth Class, has low ability levels and is from a family where dishonesty and cheating is the norm. She has low ability level as regards her work in school, and was unable to accept that she was not as good as her peers. She had developed a highly skilled method of copying her work, so that she had convinced her teachers that she could actually do what in fact was much too difficult for her. Anne was convinced that she had to get everything right to please her teachers and to 'be as good as the others' in her class.

Her way of copying was particularly well developed when it came to writing her spellings, especially if she had a spelling test. She would write the words in between her fingers, press the imprint onto the page, or simply copy from the person next to her. It is obvious that she would go to great lengths to keep up the charade of her effectiveness.

One day while she was with the remedial teacher, she asked to change her position at the table. When asked why, she became defensive and evasive. She needed to move so that the teacher could not see what she was doing. The need to get the teacher's approval and the respect of her peers was so great that she was prepared to go to any lengths to achieve this. Even though she knew what she was doing was not acceptable behaviour, it was her only way of coping.

In helping Anne to accept herself as she was, the important thing was that her teacher would accept her as she was, that the child would know this and that the pressure to measure up to the standards of others would be taken away.

This was achieved by including Anne in a process in which there was a conscious explanation of what was happening. At the same time, the need to copy was taken away. This was achieved by giving her the words in her spelling test, on a page, face down beside her on her table, and allowing her to look if she wished. This showed her that the teacher could accept her limitations and it also handed the responsibility for her action back to Anne herself. The crucial part of this process was that Anne's need to copy was taken away when she knew that her teacher knew and accepted her as she was, with her limitations.

CHAPTER 13
COMMUNICATION

The more technological communication has developed, the more isolated people have become.

Language is our principal means of communication, but it is not the only way we have of communicating. It is probably true to say that right now there is too much dependence on verbal forms of communication. Communication means all forms of sending messages, and getting information across to other people. It includes talking, laughing, crying, silence, body language, hugging, kissing, arguing, fighting and all forms of technological communication. Most of our communication takes place at the level of conscious, physical, verbal interaction. The dominance of verbal forms of interaction in our society means that the other forms of sending and receiving messages have been neglected.

We communicate unconsciously as well as consciously. Firstly, let's take a look at the importance of language in developing learned effectiveness in the child. It begins with the birth of the child and how we talk to her, whether we feel that talking to the child is important even though she may not understand. In the pre-verbal stage of the child's life, communication is more effective in a non-verbal way. That is, we should use communication by touch, facial expression and simply by intuition and tuning into the child at an imaginative level. By monitoring the child's moods and her feelings, we can gauge what is going on and can communicate more effectively with her. Often silence is a more powerful form of communication than speech. Although non-verbal communication is so important before the child learns to talk, it is in talking and singing to the child, laughing and smiling, that the child is stimulated to talk, and that she is exposed to the speech patterns and language content on which her own speech and language will be based.

Language, spoken and written, is still the basis of the child's life. It enables the child to relate to others, it helps her to establish her place in her environment and it is essential for almost all her life activities. A wide vocabulary forms the basis for much of what the child needs to do at school. Vocabulary comes from hearing, using and experimenting with words. The better the vocabulary, the better the reading, the better the communication skills and the more confident the child will be about herself.

Work patterns and life style generally have contributed in some degree to the erosion of the ability to communicate. The rise in television watching means that more time is spent in passive rather than active contact with words and language. The proliferation of playstations and computer games has also meant that more time is being spent in one-way communication with mechanical objects. Add to this to the fact that children spend less and less time playing on the street, walking to school, or in talking with parents and it is clear that most language development is taking place in the context of passive acceptance of words from a screen. Because children learn so much of their language from a mechanical device and not through interaction with people, the emotional connotation of the words is often not picked up by the child. In other words, the children know the words in a purely academic sense, but are not aware of the affect or emotion which goes with them.

This also applies to many of the behaviours which children learn from the screen. They see violent behaviour presented to them on a screen, but do not experience the emotion that accompanies it. They then repeat this behaviour in the playground and at home in the belief that it is anodyne. The effective child is one who both knows the word, and knows the literal and emotional implications of his language.

The most colourful and complex language patterns are learned in the environment where there is play, experiment and the freedom to invent. Street language may not always be acceptable in the classroom or in the home, but its complex and inventive language patterns are the essence of good communication.

The tendency to standardise speech patterns and accents is a move towards limiting the possibilities of language. Pride in oneself in one's own place is an essential part of the child developing the skills of personal effectiveness; together with this goes a pride in one's language and accent. This is a part of the process of learning to value difference and to feel that what he has is just as good as what others have. Standardisation of accents, or the erosion of the child's natural way of speaking, which can occur when children attend speech and drama or elocution classes, is giving the message to the child that the accent the child speaks with normally is deficient or inferior.

Language is empowering, both for children and adults, and the ability to use it well conveys to the child a sense of competence and mastery of her environment. Not allowing a child to answer for herself, speaking for her and not listening to her, inhibit her use of language and limit the development of her language skills. The communication system used in the home is not only the one which will be the model which the child will use later, but it also determines much of how the child communicates, deals with conflict and resolves disagreements. If it is an open system where all the people in the group have a chance to speak and where listening is as important as talking, then the child will learn that she doesn't have to shout to be heard and she will also learn that she can have her say and that it matters. However, if it is a closed and rigid system where conversation and discussion are discouraged and where there is only one voice that counts, then the model the child will have is one of helplessness and disempowerment. In this case, she will feel that what she has to say is of no value and she will not get the opportunity to develop her language skills.

The vocabulary of negotiation is different from the vocabulary of confrontation and it is something that is learnt and taught. If the family model is one of confrontation, then the child will pick it up and use it.

Many parents and teachers find the children's use of 'bad' language to be very upsetting and distasteful, but it is nevertheless a form of language and is therefore a form of communication. It is important to note that in using bad language the child is trying to get a message across. In choosing to use such language, the child is choosing a social skill which she has learned to be necessary for survival in her environment. The fact that she chooses to use a form of language which is not acceptable is in itself saying something. It is often the child's way of showing off her newly acquired skill, and our reaction as parents and teachers will often determine the importance the child attaches to bad language. So when a child uses bad language, we look at how she says it as well as what she says. But remember they are words first and foremost, and our reaction will probably determine whether the child uses them again. If we overreact, then this may be the response that the child wants and it will prompt her to do it again. In many cases, what happens is that the adult projects his own emotional memories onto the words which the child is using, and they take on a much more negative and distasteful meaning than the child intended. Very often, if parents and teachers demystify the words being used by the child and allow the child to see that they are not shocked by them, it takes away the power which the child derives from these words. It also takes away some of the need which the child has to use them. Where the child is using slang or obscene words denoting parts of the body, it can be useful in disempowering the words if parents or teachers are not shocked and teach the child other, more technically correct, words.

Showing disapproval, that it is not our 'usual mode of communication', and by not depending on 'bad' language in the normal life situations, is sufficient to dissuade the child from dependence on using bad language. As in everything else, it is our 'usual way of being' which is the model for our children's behaviour and which is most instrumental in how they behave. But like it or not, there are situations in which 'bad' language is useful. There are situations in a child's life where she may need to use strong language, to assert herself or to survive in her own world. She needs to know that while using bad language is not the usual way of communicating 'in this family', and that while it may not be the most acceptable way of dealing with a situation, at the same time it can be useful and she should have the ability to use it when necessary. Where a child has an exaggerated emotional aversion to 'bad' language, he is vulnerable to other people abusing him through the use of bad language.

In addition to verbal communication, parents and teachers should develop and promote other forms of communication. There is a tendency to over-rely on the written and spoken word. In the process, other forms of communication are being overlooked. Children communicate with parents in many other ways and it is helpful to be tuned in to the child's feelings, moods and tantrums. By being aware of the child's dreams and nightmares, the parent can have an insight into the inner world of the child. Another way in which the child sends messages to his parents is during play, when children will often act out the anxieties and conflicts which are often otherwise hidden from view. The most important part of communication is to be sure that the signals being sent are also the messages being received.

Communication and the Effective Child: The Parents' Role

Talk is the basis of all communication and it is the main form of telling others what we are thinking and the main method of knowing about other people and their needs. Unfortunately, due to the way our world has changed, due to the social, religious and historical inheritance, there is a tendency to talk to other people rather than talk with them. This is especially the case in the verbal interaction between adults and children, where there is also an authority or supervisory aspect to the relationship. Talking with the child means being there with the child both physically and psychologically at the time. It means looking at the child as we speak and treating the child as an equal in the conversation.

Listening is the other half of the verbal equation and while talking with a child is important, it is nothing unless we also listen to and hear what the child is saying. Active listening, where the child knows by our body language and our reactions that we have heard and are taking account of what she has said to us, is the basis for effective communication.

A very useful strategy in encouraging children to talk and to listen is circle time. It also helps to develop the skill of allowing others to have their say. One of the most important feelings for people in general, and for children especially, is the feeling that they have a say, have a role to play and are a part of what is happening to them. This makes them feel included and empowered and helps them to be effective in the conduct of their own lives. They need not only to have a say, but to have something to say and to feel able to say it. Circle time provides the opportunity to practise this skill. But it is also important for the child to know and accept that the other people in his world also have a say and that it is not a threat to him when they talk.

Language improves with practice, and the more a child uses words and language generally the more developed his verbal ability will become. Parents can help this process by:

- Playing word games.
- Talking about television programmes.
- Encouraging and answering questions.
- Having lots of non-mechanical toys that the child can fantasise and talk about.
- Having a family pet.
- Talking about the child's reading.
- Turning off the television during meal times.
- Telling stories.
- Reading.

Communication and the Effective Child: The Teacher's Role

Circle time is particularly appropriate for the classroom situation as a means of developing communication skills, verbal ability and self-esteem and in dealing with such problems as bullying and disruptive behaviour. It is helpful if there is a school policy about using circle time and that it is an accepted part of the week's work.

Asking questions requires verbal ability and confidence and it is therefore a skill, which must be modelled, nurtured and facilitated. The teacher can do this by reacting positively to questions, by modelling good questioning technique and encouraging a climate of questioning among the children.

Talking in class has tended to have a bad press among teachers, parents and society generally, and perhaps schools can look at ways of creating a positive attitude towards talk. One way to do this might be to have a 'talk time' during the day. When the children meet for the first time each morning, they enjoy sharing their experiences and it is therefore a good time for 'talk time'.

In teaching the child skills for effective communication, the way in which we use language and the type of language we use are both important. If a teacher more usually uses language which is highly structured, closed and logical, this will convey a logical bias in thinking to the children and will mean that the child will replicate such language and thinking. If the teacher uses language which is open, inclusive and receptive, he will convey this type of thinking to the child. The more soft, feeling type of language invites involvement, and lends itself to developing relationships and connections more than the hard, clinical language of logic.

THINGS TO WATCH FOR

- The child who talks all the time.
- The child who never talks.
- The child who uses 'age inappropriate' language.

155

- The child who hides (tries to be unobtrusive) in the class or in the house.
- The child who can't express his feelings.
- The child who clams up when things go wrong.

Liam's Story

Liam is twenty-five, the oldest of three children. He is a tall, well-built and physically strong young man who conveys the impression of being brave and unafraid. His father was always domineering towards Liam and physically beat him, right up to the present time. Liam's negative father complex was so strong and powerful that all his energy and power had been siphoned out by his father. His father would not allow him to make any decisions for himself, would not give credit for any achievements and constantly criticised and put him down. Although Liam had his own business and was financially independent, he became depressed and at times suicidal, felt he had no say in what happened to him, and had no feeling that the future had anything to give him. He was emotionally crippled by his strong, negative emotional attachment to his father. His father's emotional dominance meant that Liam could not live with his father, but had not yet developed the skills to live without him. This story is complicated by the fact that Liam's father was not able to let go of him, because his son was the only person in his life that he could be sure of.

The turning point for Liam was when he painted a picture of his depression. What he painted was a picture of a man being weighed down by a heavy load. Painting his depression enabled Liam to externalise it and to put it out in the open. He began to feel that he could have some control over it and therefore that he could begin to challenge his father's emotional dominance.

CHAPTER 14
THE SHADOW OF PERFECTION

Seeking perfection in our children hides our own unhappiness with ourselves.

The constant search for the perfect home with the perfect children all taken care of by the perfect parents is a feature of our society today. This search for perfection in society is generated by a deep, unconscious dissatisfaction with the self. It is fuelled by constant television and media reinforcement of the always clean, happy, well dressed and perfectly shaped person.

Because this unhappiness is unconscious, the person is not aware of it and it manifests itself in the person's life as a constant struggle to have everything appearing to be perfect. This desire for perfection includes the children. Perfectionism happens in the following way. A parent wants to fulfil unlived ambitions and tries to do this through the child. By idealising, that is conferring 'special' or 'perfect' status on the child, the parent demands that the child has to be perfect to get approval. If he fails, he is punished by not being loved. The child will naturally try to please the parent, which means always trying to be perfect. The child gradually internalises this need to please and even when the parent is no longer an active part of the child's life, this quest for approval/perfection is part of the child's psychological makeup. It manifests in the following ways:

- He cannot bear to get something wrong.
- He is not able to take criticism.
- He is never satisfied with himself or his performance.

- He is too close to the parent emotionally.
- He will always check before doing something.
- He will find it difficult to make decisions.
- He will always seek to please others rather than having opinions of his own.
- He will be passive and over-compliant.
- When not passive, he will be aggressive and selfish.
- He finds it difficult to concentrate on what he is doing now.
- He will always be thinking of what he is going to do next.

Perfectionism in parents is characterised by a never-ending search for the unattainable, often projected onto the child. The parents' continuous searching and unease with themselves becomes transferred to the child, who can never achieve objectives which are unattainable, for lots of reasons. Firstly, they are unattainable for the child because they are unstated and unconscious for the parents. Secondly, they are unattainable because perfectionism is an idea which is not realisable in the real world. Thirdly, these objectives are unattainable for the child because they relate to people outside himself and are not based on his own needs and aptitudes.

Perfectionism is an idea which cannot become a reality, and the constant searching for something which we really know to be unattainable is merely a way of hiding our own unconscious feelings of inadequacy from ourselves. It is a defence mechanism, a way of avoiding the painful experience of our own feelings of inadequacy. By constantly searching for perfection in the conscious world, in the world of objects, materialism and achievement, we are avoiding facing up to our feelings of inadequacy. Of course, the longer we pursue the unattainable, the longer we can put off the unpleasant task of confronting our own shadow. It is as if we feel that we are doing something about it, so everything is all right.

Where our children are concerned, something more serious occurs. In constantly seeking the unattainable, we are receiving negative feedback about ourselves and projecting both the search for perfection and its negative baggage onto our children. The children internalise this as their own failure, and the feelings of inadequacy are exaggerated because they feel they are letting their parents down by not fulfilling their expectations.

This addiction to perfection is only one of the many forms of addiction through which we avoid dealing both with ourselves and with others. The addiction to work, that is the workaholic, is another avoidance strategy used to hide from the unpleasant task of relationships and feelings by burying oneself in work.

The 'human doing' approach, where there is a constant need to be active, going somewhere or involved in some form of activity, is being transmitted to children. It results in an 'addiction to distraction', where we always need to have something happening. We see this in the way in which children and adults always need to have music playing, the television on, or to be doing something. This has the effect of not allowing people to learn about themselves, not being at ease with themselves. It creates the idea that unless one is actually doing something, there is something wrong. This is what is called the human doing approach to life, where there is all doing and no time for being.

The effect on the child is that he learns that the correct way of living is always to be doing something. The ability to relax is learned through seeing other people relaxing and realising that it is acceptable to take it easy sometimes. If the parents are always busy, always thinking of the next thing to be done and never able to live in the 'now', children do not get the level of attention they need and they learn that relaxing is wrong.

The Perfect Parent

The perfect parent is the one who never makes a mistake, who never forgets to pick her child up from school and is always available for the child. The kitchen is never untidy and the children are always neat, clean and tidy. In the world of the perfect parent, there is no room for being late, making mistakes or making a mess. The perfect parent is always there for the child, always has the answers and tries to send out conscious signals that everything is perfect and that anything less than perfection is failure.

The perfect parent is nothing more than a myth perpetuated by a television image of modern life, which portrays both people and home as being always neat, clean and tidy. It preys on people's need for affiliation and creates the impression that somehow if we can have neat, clean and tidy lives, we will have gained acceptance with friends and colleagues, and that clean, neat, tidy lives on the outside means the same thing inside.

The effect on children is that they become budding perfectionists themselves. The model of perfectionism that is being presented as the model of best practice is the model on which they base their own view of life. We see this in action with the five-year-old child who cannot cope with the idea of getting something wrong in school, and who is crippled by the fear of making a mistake. The worry and anxiety which such a child experiences simply because he is afraid to make a mistake, or because he feels that his parents/teachers will be displeased with his work, becomes a barrier to growth and achievement.

The Perfect Teacher

The perfect teacher always has order in the classroom. The children's work is always perfectly presented. He never needs help or advice, because everything is perfect. When a child makes a mistake, it is seen as a personal slight on the teacher and in general mistakes are not acceptable, either the children's or the teacher's mistakes. The perfect teacher always has the answer and never has a problem, and of course works in the perfect classroom.

So how does the child see it? In the perfect classroom, the child is afraid to make a mistake and very often will not try until he is sure of getting it right. He will not make a decision until he knows that his teacher agrees with it.

An important aspect of the whole idea of school is teaching children that it is OK to make a mistake, and as a result they can learn that they have limits. Where there is a model of perfectionism being presented to the child, he does not learn his limitations and will find it difficult to form a realistic concept of himself. Being able to cope with making a mistake, knowing that making a mistake is not an assessment of him as a person and being able to get on with it after the mistake, are important issues in the growth and development of the child. Where the model presented to the child is one of perfectionism, he will not be able to do any of these things and will seek perfection as the only way of achieving satisfaction.

The Perfect Child

The perfect child never gets his clothes dirty and always has his room tidy, with everything in its proper place. His schoolwork is always neat and tidy and he never gets anything wrong. If he does, it will be rubbed out and hidden so that it will appear that he never makes mistakes. He never breaks the rules and always does what he is told. He never questions things and always asks for permission before doing anything or going anywhere. In short, he is a 'good boy'.

Good-Enough Will Do

The concept of the good-enough parent is one which has been around for some time, but has not yet been accepted. What it means is that the parent accepts that she is not perfect and cannot be, and that even if it were possible, she has rejected the idea of perfection.

The good-enough parent is one who accepts both himself and those around him for who they are. He accepts both himself and his child as fallible, sometimes untidy, sometimes late. The good-enough parent knows that people make mistakes and that mistakes are the springboard for growth and development. He knows that he himself will often get it wrong and that his child will notice this, but he has no difficulty in admitting this to his child. He is never right 'just because I say so'.

This ability to be wrong is part of the good-enough parent's approach to school and school work. Home work does not have to be perfect, neat, tidy and correct. The good-enough parent operates in the world of the second chance, where learning is more process than product and where there is always another chance to do something.

The good-enough parent is a parent who can take the child as he finds him. He can allow the child the space to make mistakes and the support to deal with the mistake so that the child will not grow up with the idea that a mistake somehow makes him an inferior person. The good-enough parent feels happy enough with himself so that he can allow the child to make decisions, and he doesn't feel that he always has to have a say in what his child does. He has no problem standing back and allowing the child to take credit for success or responsibility for 'failure'.

In much the same way, the idea of the good-enough teacher applies. It involves accepting that mistakes are normal and that the child is not perfect. The good-enough teacher is able to accept his own limitations and because of this, he can accept the limitations of the child.

Perfectionism and the Effective Child: The Parents' Role

If families have a quiet time in the house, where 'doing nothing' is encouraged, it will give you a chance to see what your inner thoughts are. It will allow the child to have space and time to be by himself, and to learn that it is sometimes acceptable to do nothing.

It sometimes happens that an excessive emphasis on order, neatness and tidiness can interfere with getting things done. It can cause the seeds of perfectionism to be sown in the child and can lead to an underlying unhappiness with oneself which worsens as the child grows into adulthood. Appearance and image become internalised as the criteria for success, at the expense of substance and content. If parents can lower their standards as regards neatness, tidiness and order in the house, it will help the child in lots of ways. It will particularly help the child to develop a 'good-enough' attitude to himself, his life and his immediate social environment.

Untidiness is not a fault, it is more a manifestation of a particular type of personality, and while 'tidying your room' is a necessary chore, a healthy attitude to tidiness and untidiness will help the child to develop a balance between perfection and reality.

If parents can take a softer line on making a mess, it will allow the child to be more at ease in her environment, it will help the child to achieve more, and it will teach her a healthier attitude to achievement and standards.

Recreation and play are usually unpredictable and unorganised and if parents have a positive attitude to play, if they take part in recreation and play themselves, it will have two major benefits for the children. It will convey the message that it is OK, and more importantly, it will legitimise a more tolerant and creative attitude to life. It is important that parents take time out for recreation with and without their children.

Deferred gratification, and long-term plans, show that it is acceptable to wait for something, that it doesn't have to be right now and it helps to avoid becoming a slave to perfectionism.

Much of our creativity arises out of mistakes that have led to taking another look at something, and if parents can adopt the view that the mistake is the opportunity, they will provide the child with space and freedom to become creative. A 'mistake is the opportunity' approach to your child and his work will also allow the child to develop a positive attitude to his own flaws and limitations and will provide the child with a guilt-free approach to learning. If parents can approach their child's mistakes in a non-judgmental way, it will help the child to have a reality based attitude to learning and to life and will protect him against being ruled by the need to do things perfectly.

Perfectionism and the Effective Child: The Teachers' Role

The role and the responsibility of the teacher is as much to facilitate learning as it is to teach. As with parenting, teaching is a complex mix of providing information for the child and enabling the child to find it himself, mediated through the personality and skill of the teacher. For the teacher, constrained as he is by numbers, curricular demands and individual needs, it is especially demanding to treat the children's mistakes as opportunities. But the classroom is a particularly appropriate arena in which to do this, as it is the place most associated in the child's mind, and in the parent's mind, with learning.

Perfectionism is to a considerable extent an unconscious process and for the most part adults may be unaware that they are perfectionists. Given the nature and context of teaching, it is easy for a teacher who has perfectionist tendencies to thrive and indeed to be perceived as a 'good' teacher. It is therefore essential that a teacher becomes conscious of her own personality and is aware of any tendencies towards perfectionism, to ensure that these are not projected on to the children she is working with.

The teacher can offer special encouragement to the child by being conscious of the content of the child's work as well as the look of it. The context of the school is one where order and structure are often paramount and it is important that school authorities do not become too fixated on the importance of appearance.

A quiet time can help both teacher and child to take time out from the rush to get things done and from the pressure to have things right. It can be worthwhile to set aside a time each day for quiet and doing nothing.

Playtime is the time during the day when children feel that they are allowed to be uninhibited and free. While taking into account the demands of insurance and safety, schools should try to make sure that playtime is as free from adult interference as possible. Where adults intervene in children's play, a sense of structure, order and 'performing' is introduced and the play becomes an adjunct of the classroom, with 'school' priorities operating.

Be aware of the child who has perfectionist traits. He may be carrying these traits from one or both of his parents, or indeed he may be responding to the unconscious transmission of perfectionist ideas from the teacher. It is helpful if the teacher can make space for him and give him the chance to make mistakes, to make a mess without causing fear and anxiety.

A child who always asks permission before attempting something may be showing the beginnings of perfectionism and if the teacher can be conscious of this, he will be able to develop a relationship where the child will begin to shed his perfectionism. This is also true of the child who is overly compliant and obedient, sometimes mistakenly referred to as a 'good' boy. Over-compliance and over-obedience, while perhaps the result of severe lack of confidence in oneself, may also be a sign that the child is afraid to take a chance in case it won't be 'right'.

THINGS TO WATCH FOR

- The child who gets overly upset when he makes a mistake.
- The child who never steps out of line.
- The child who is overly compliant.
- The child who is afraid to show his mistakes.
- The child who cannot take criticism.
- The child who finds it difficult to deal with name calling and teasing.

Niall's Story

Niall is the oldest in a family of three. He is at university, a brilliant musician, and wants to drop out. His parents are successful people and would like Niall to be successful. Niall's view of success does not match his parents' view.

As a young child, Niall was brought everywhere, collected and not allowed to go his own way at any time. His parents always demanded to know where he was. Everything about him was expected to be perfect — his behaviour, his appearance and his work. He lived with a family where everything was planned, controlled and where all outcomes could be predicted.

No matter how well he performed in school or at home, it was not enough to satisfy his parents. They always wanted more. Niall gradually realised that no matter what he did, or how well he did it, his parents would not be satisfied. To Niall, this meant that he could never gain the parental approval which is so important to the development of self-esteem. Because the goals he was seeking to achieve were not his own, he could never experience the achievement satisfaction which normally goes with personal achievement.

Niall responded to his parents' excessive control and protection by resorting to the most effective means at his disposal, of rejecting and shutting them out. He became deceitful and secretive and would not share his experiences with his parents, or ask for their help. It was his way of trying to break free from the constricting binds of his parents' perfectionism.

If Niall's parents can bring their perfection to consciousness, and become aware of Niall's needs as being separate from their own unconscious need to keep satisfying their own emotional greed, it will be possible for Niall to achieve his own objectives. This will not come in a blinding flash of realisation, but through personal growth. At the same time, Niall will learn that his own needs and goals are valid in their own right and he does not have to hide them behind deceit and lies.

CHAPTER 15
THE EFFECTIVE CHILD

The prevalence of abuse cases and the legitimate and necessary concerns which parents have for their children's welfare often become confused with unjustified fears and exaggerated caution. Perception and reality have become blurred where the child's safety is concerned, and by overprotecting children, society is preventing them from developing their survival skills.

Overprotection stifles growth, because it takes away opportunities to make decisions, to solve disputes, to choose, to deal with one's own life situations. If we don't allow children the opportunity to acquire and practise the skills of the effective child, then they will not have them when they need them, and will have no practice at using them. When they encounter people who have them, they will be unable to cope, and will react by becoming overly defensive or overly aggressive.

There is a natural tendency to protect, to take care of the vulnerable and to look after our children, both because we care about them as people and because it is our way of safeguarding our future. When our unconscious anxiety about safeguarding the future remains unconscious, it can dominate our thinking. We are then in danger of overprotecting in the mistaken belief that that what we are doing is in the best interests of the child. In this case, it is really the parents' own needs which take precedence and which are the motivating force behind the behaviour of the parents and teachers.

Overprotection manifests as:

- Too much supervision.
- Bringing children to school, not allowing the child to go to school with his friends.
- Supervising them at play.
- Driving children to after-school activities.
- Not allowing children to play by themselves.
- Doing too much for our children, dressing them, feeding them, doing their homework, tidying up after them.
- Not allowing the child to have his own opinions.
- Not believing your child.
- Interfering in your child's arguments.
- Not letting your child out to play.
- Being afraid to let your child stay overnight in a friend's house.
- Anxiety about the child whenever he is away.
- Feeling uneasy about letting somebody else look after your child.
- Choosing your child's friends.

The main effects of overprotection are that the child is not allowed to face up to her own life situations and to develop the skills that she will need in handling these situations. These are skills that she has the capacity to develop if she is given the right growth conditions. They are the skills that she develops in the family, in school, in the playground and on the street and which she needs when she leaves the protection of the family and the school. They are the skills of the effective child.

It is by being allowed to learn, use and practise them that a child becomes adept in the use of the social, emotional and physical skills which are the building blocks of the effective child.

The skills of the effective child are the ability to:

- Interact, to argue and debate with peers.
- Accept the other person's point of view.
- Accept that she can't always win.
- Negotiate.
- Say how he feels.
- Share sadness and happiness.
- Have sympathy.
- Own his anger, sadness, joy without feeling ashamed.
- Be aware of her body and its capabilities.
- Share his personal space without feeling threatened.
- Assert her position without being aggressive.
- Know what he is capable of and what he is not capable of.
- Take risks.
- Take credit for success.

It also involves the confidence to fail and the willingness to try. These are skills which are best acquired and practised in the real world of their peers, with parents and teachers playing no more than a supporting role. They are the skills which make up the overall package of personal effectiveness. It is the aspiration that our children should have these skills which is important. It is the process of acquiring them which brings growth and development to a family.

By overprotecting and overcosseting the child, we deny him the chance to acquire and to practise these skills and if he is never allowed to use them, then the skills remain latent, become dormant and eventually become extinguished.

Children who are overprotected never manage to find out their capabilities and never discover their limits. They are not allowed to test themselves against the realities of the outside world, and they do not get the opportunity to flex their emotional and social muscles in the unprotected world of their peers. So they never find out how good they really are, or how limited they are. This means that they don't develop the knowledge of their capability, which is essential if they are to be able to take on assignments on their own. The effective child is one who knows her capabilities and accepts her limitations.

Overprotection means that the child will always check before doing something. He will become dependent on the judgment of the parent or the teacher before he acts and he never learns to trust his own judgment. This means that the child is unable to form an accurate or realistic concept of self, which is an intrinsic element in building his self-esteem. In fostering personal effectiveness, it is essential that the child have the chance to test his judgment and to experience the satisfaction of getting it right, as well as having to live with the consequences of getting it wrong.

Decision making is based on confidence in one's own judgment, the knowledge that the significant adults in your life think you can do it and that the consequences of your possible failure are not too much of a threat to your own self-view. Where the parent overprotects the child, all of these are taken out of the hands of the child and the message she receives is that the parents do not consider her capable of carrying out the task. The child internalises this view and it becomes the deciding factor in the way in which she deals with all her life situations. She is unwilling to take the risk of being wrong, and she never learns that she has the ability to make decisions and therefore never learns 'how' to make decisions. The effective child has learned the implications of decision making and can live with them.

In this situation, the willingness to try and the confidence to fail which go hand-in-hand in the development of achievement and mastery skills, are not developed, as the child won't risk the damage to his sense of self which he associates with failure. Consequently, because he won't try, he does not experience the satisfaction that goes with achievement. The effective child knows that he may not always get it right and accepts this about himself, and consequently is willing to try and happy to fail.

Each child has the innate capability to survive and to cope adequately with all his life situations, even though these capabilities are latent and need to be fostered and encouraged. But this involves facilitation rather than direct intervention. It involves allowing the child the opportunity to use and practise the skills of the effective child, rather than trying to 'do' it for them. The effective child is one who is competent to face up to the challenges, both personal and social, which she encounters.

Argument is a legitimate and useful form of communication and it is important in teaching the child the value of both expressing and accepting opinion. The tendency to see arguing and disagreement as being negative and something to be avoided often leads to parents and teachers interfering in and stopping children's arguments. While reason should prevail, the effective child is a child who can have an argument, and so can learn the value of his own opinion in the overall context of his world. At times of stress or difficulty, we often revert to the successful survival strategies of childhood and become either very aggressive or very passive to achieve our ends. The effective child will know how to get his point across without having to resort to this form of aggression, because he will have experienced effective communication based on knowing the value of what he has to say, as well as the value of what the other person has to say.

The effective child feels secure, because she knows that she belongs to a group which values her for who she is. She feels accepted by the adults in her life, and her sense of identity is supported by knowing that she is included, regardless of what she does.

The effective child is emotionally literate. He can express feelings, and feels comfortable when others express feelings. He knows the vocabulary of feelings and emotions and is able to accept and give praise. He doesn't feel threatened when others are praised, and can accept criticism. He is a child who has confidence in himself to do things and to achieve, and yet he knows that there is a possibility that he may fail. He knows that he has potential and that he has limits.

The effective child is one who is proud of his family, his community and his country and does not feel threatened by the success of others. He is at ease with his own view of himself and feels accepted by those around him. He does not see criticism as rejection. He is always willing to try, though he knows there is a possibility of 'failure'. He trusts the judgment of those around him, but is not afraid to exercise his own judgment. He can survive emotionally and physically with his parents and without them.

BIBLIOGRAPHY

Bosnak, R., *A Little Course in Dreams*, Boston: Shambhala, 1988

Burns, Robert, *Self Concept and Education*, London/New York: Holt Rinehart and Winston, 1982

Colman, A. and Colman, L., *The Father: Mythology and Changing Roles*, Wilmette, Illinois: Chiron Publications, 1988

Coopersmith, S., *The Antecedents of Self-Esteem*, San Francisco: Freeman Press, 1967

Crisp, A. H., *Anorexia Nervosa: Let me Be*, London: Baillière Tindall, 1990

Davis, M., and Wallbridge, D., *Boundary and Space: An Introduction to the work of D. W. Winnicott*, London: Karnac, 1981

Fordham, F., *An Introduction to Jung's Psychology*, London: Penguin, 1990

Gardner, H., *The Theory of Multiple Intelligences*, London: Fontana, 1993

Henderson, N., 'Human Behaviour Genetics' in *Annual Review of Psychology*, (33), pp 403–40, 1982

Kagan, J., *The Nature of the Child*, New York: Basic Books, 1984

Kagan, J., and Moss, H. A., *Birth to Maturity*, New York: John Wiley, 1962

Konig, K., *Brothers and Sisters: The Order of Birth in the Family*, Edinburgh: Floris Books, 1993

Kottman, T., *Partners in Play: An Adlerian Approach to Play Therapy*, Alexandria, Virginia: American Counselling Association, 1995

Jacobs, M., *D. W. Winnicott*, London: Sage, 1995

Jung, C. G., *Dictionary of Analytical Psychology*, London: Ark, 1971

Jung, C. G., *On the Nature of the Psyche*, London: Ark, 1969

Lawrence, D., *Enhancing Self-Esteem in the Classroom*, London: Paul Chapman Publishing, 1987

Lochlin, J. C., *Heredity, Environment and Personality*, Austin: University of Texas Press, 1976

Matson, J. L., *Treating Depression in Children and Adolescents*, New York, Oxford: Pergamon Press, 1989

Meier, C.A., *Personality: The Individuation Process in the Light of C.G. Jung's Typology*, Einsiedeln, Switzerland: Daimon, 1995

Mitchell, J., *The Selected Melanie Klein*, London: Penguin, 1986

Mussen, P. H., *Handbook of Child Psychology*, New York: Wiley, 1983

Neuman, E., *The Child*, London: Karnac, 1973

Oaklander, V., *Windows to our Children*, New York: Gestalt Journal Press, 1988

O Donnchadha, R., *Self-Actualisation in the Classroom*, Dublin: E.T.C. Consult, 1996

Postman, N., *Amusing Ourselves to Death*, London: Heinemann, 1986

Read, H., Fordham, M., Adler, G., and Mc Guire, W. (Eds), *C.G. Jung: Two Essays in Analytical Psychology*, (Translated by R. F. C. Hull) New York: Princeton University Press, 1977

Reasoner, Robert W., *Building Self-Esteem: A Parent's Guide*, Palo Alto, California: Consulting Psychologists Press, 1982

Rose, R. J., Harris, E. L., and Christian, J. C., *Genetic Variance in Non-Verbal Intelligence: Data for Kinships of Identical Twins*, Science 205:1153-1155, 1979

Santrock, J.W., *Child Development: An Introduction*, Dubuque, Iowa: Wm C. Browne Publishers, 1987

Sidoli, M. and Davies, M., *Jungian Child Psychotherapy*, London: Karnac, 1988

Singer, J., *Boundaries of the Soul*, New York, London: Anchor Books, Doubleday, 1994

Springer, S.P. and Deutsch, G., *Left Brain: Right Brain*, New York: W.H. Freeman and Co., 1993

St Clair, M., *Object Relations and Self-Psychology*, Monterey: Brooks' Cole Publishing, 1986

Taylor, C., *The Explanation of Behaviour*, London: Routledge and Kegan Paul, 1980

Varma, P. V., *The Management of Children with Emotional and Behavioural Difficulties*, London: Routledge, 1990

Vitale, B. M., *Unicorns are Real*, Torrance, California: Jalmar Press, 1982

Weininger, O., *Children's Fantasies: The Shaping of Relationships*, London: Karnac, 1989

Westwood, P., *Commonsense Methods for Children with Special Needs*, London: Routledge, 1987

Wickes, F. G., *The Inner World of Man*, Boston: Sigo, 1988

Winnicott, D. W., *Playing and Reality*, London: Routledge, 1971